Pelican Books

with additional texts by
Clement Greenberg
Michael Fried
John Russell
Phyllis Tuchman

Richard Whelan was born in New York. He graduated from Yale in
1969 and remained there to do one year's graduate work in art history
and Chinese. He is currently living in New York, working at the
New York Public Library, and he has recently completed a survey of
scatological imagery in Western art and literature.

Penguin Books

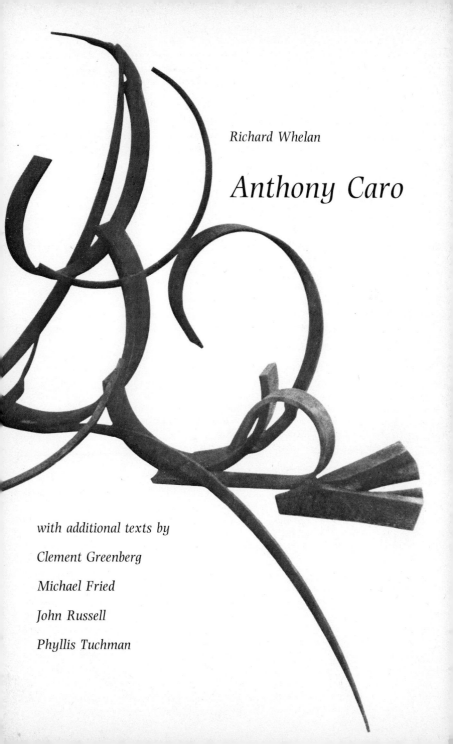

Richard Whelan

Anthony Caro

with additional texts by

Clement Greenberg

Michael Fried

John Russell

Phyllis Tuchman

Penguin Books Ltd, Harmondsworth, Middlesex, England
Penguin Books Inc., 7110 Ambassador Road, Baltimore, Maryland 21207, U.S.A.
Penguin Books Australia Ltd, Ringwood, Victoria, Australia

First published 1974

Filmset by Oliver Burridge Filmsetting Ltd
and printed in Great Britain
at the University Press, Oxford
by Vivian Ridler
Printer to the University

Set in Monophoto Photina

Designed by Gerald Cinamon

Editorial Foreword

Richard Whelan was originally commissioned to write a monograph on Anthony Caro for the Penguin New Art Series, edited by Richard Morphet; this book was to have been published in the format of the other titles in that series.

It was later decided, however, to proceed with the book in a way different from the one originally envisaged: I felt it would be best to add to Richard Whelan's text (which originated as a thesis at Yale University) a number of articles by different authors who often expressed different points of view, sometimes even contradictory to those of Richard Whelan. I feel that the advantage in doing so is in communicating to the reader a dialectically richer sense of Caro's work. The additional articles I have chosen to include have all been published previously in art magazines and exhibition catalogues and are not readily available except to the specialist. This supplementary material is now part of the standard bibliography on Caro's sculpture and we think it is valuable enough to give it a more permanent stature by including it in this book. Richard Whelan's text was completed in July 1970. Through no fault of his, it is only published now.

Clement Greenberg's article first appeared in *The Art Digest, Contemporary Sculpture*, Arts Yearbook 8, New York, 1965. It was included in the catalogue text of Caro's Kröller-Müller exhibition in Holland, in 1967, and was also published in *Studio International*, London, September 1967.

Michael Fried's 'Two Sculptures by Anthony Caro' was first published in *Artforum* in February 1968. His second article, 'Caro's Abstractness', also appeared in *Artforum*, September 1970.

John Russell's 'Closing the Gaps' was first published in *Art News*, Vol. 69, No. 3, May 1970.

Phyllis Tuchman's interview (started in 1970 and completed in 1971) first appeared in *Artforum*, June 1972.

Grateful acknowledgement is due to the authors of these articles and to the editors of the publications where they first appeared, for allowing us to reprint them in this book.

We would also like to thank the Kasmin Gallery, London, and the André Emmerich Gallery, New York, for providing many of the photographs.

Finally, I should like to thank warmly Gerald Cinamon without whose valuable assistance and meticulous care in selecting the photographs, preparing the list of illustrations and designing this book in a way which is original, functional and ideally accommodating to its material, I doubt that publication would have been possible.

Nikos Stangos

List of Illustrations

The order of measurements is as follows: height, length, width

17. *Wide*, 1964. Steel and aluminum, painted burgundy, $58\frac{1}{4}$ x 60 x 160 in. Private collection, Buffalo, N.Y. (photo: John Webb).

18. *Shaftsbury*, 1965 (U.S. sculpture). Steel painted purple, 27 x 127 x 108 in. Private collection, Boston (photo: John Webb).

19. *Smoulder*, 1965 (U.S. sculpture). Steel painted purple, 42 x 183 x 33 in. Collection: T. M. and G. P. Caro, London (photo: John Goldblatt).

20. *Eyelit*, 1965 (U.S. sculpture). Steel painted blue, $112\frac{1}{2}$ x 66 x 3 in. Collection: Mr and Mrs William S. Ehrlich. New York (photo: André Emmerich).

21. *Slow Movement*, 1965. Steel painted deep blue, 51 x 105 x 60 in. Collection: Arts Council of Great Britain (photo: John Goldblatt).

22. *Strip*, 1965. Steel and aluminum, painted red, 7 x 3 x $78\frac{3}{4}$ in. Private collection, London (photo: John Goldblatt).

23. *Away*, 1966. Steel painted blue, $40\frac{1}{2}$ x 208 x 33 in. Collection: Museum of Modern Art, New York (photo: John Goldblatt).

24. *Red Splash*, 1966. Steel painted red, $45\frac{1}{2}$ x 69 x 41 in. Collection: David Mirvish Gallery, Toronto (photo: John Webb).

25. *Carriage*, 1966. Steel painted blue, 77 x 80 x 156 in. Collection: Mr and Mrs Henry Feiwel, Larchmont, New York (photo: John Webb).

26. *Horizon*, 1966. Steel painted brown, $69\frac{1}{2}$ x 165 x 33 in. Collection: Brandeis University Art Collection, Gift of Mr and Mrs Max Wasserman (photo: John Webb).

27. *Span*, 1966. Steel painted burgundy, $77\frac{1}{2}$ x 184 x 132 in. Private collection, Boston (photo: Geoffrey Clements).

28. *The Window*, 1966–7. Steel painted two greens, $84\frac{1}{2}$ x $126\frac{3}{8}$ x $153\frac{1}{2}$ in. Collection: S. M. Caro, London (photo: Guy Martin).

29. *Prairie*, 1967. Steel painted matte yellow ochre, 38 x 229 x 126 in. Private collection, Boston (cf. illustration 43); (photo: John Goldblatt).

30. *Table Piece XVIII*, 1967. Polished steel, 10 x 21 x 20 in. Collection: Mr Kenneth Noland, New York (photo: John Goldblatt).

31. *Table Piece XXII*, 1967. Steel painted green, 10 x $31\frac{1}{2}$ x 27 in. Collection: T. M. and P. G. Caro, London (photo: John Goldblatt).

32. *Table Piece XLII*, 1967. Steel, polished and glazed green, $23\frac{1}{2}$ x $15\frac{1}{2}$ x 29 in. Collection: S. M. Caro, London (photo: John Goldblatt).

33. *Argentine*, 1968. Steel painted purple, 59 x 140 x 124 in. Collection: Mr and Mrs Henry Feiwel, Larchmont, New York (photo: Guy Martin).

34. *Trefoil*, 1968. Steel painted yellow ochre, 83 x 100 x 65 in. Private collection, Boston (photo: John Webb).

35. *Table Piece LXIV*, 1968. Steel painted matte yellow, 30 x 51 x 32 in. Collection: Mr and Mrs Clement Greenberg, New York (photo: Guy Martin).

36A. *After Summer*, in construction, 1968 (photo: John Webb).

36B. *After Summer*, 1968. Steel painted grey, 62 x 288 x 236 in. Collection: David Mirvish Gallery, Toronto (photo: R. McMillan).

37. *Table Piece LXXV*, 1969. Steel painted tan, $11\frac{1}{2}$ x 28 x 39 in. Collection: S. M. Caro, London (photo: Guy Martin).

38. *Table Piece LXXXVIII*, 1969. Steel painted matte yellow, 40 x 63 x 38 in. Collection: Mr Guido Goldman, Boston (photo: Guy Martin).

39. *Sculpture Two*, 1962 (cf. illustration 8; photo: Kim Lim).

40. *Titan*, 1964 (cf. illustration 15); (photo: John Webb).
41. *Bennington*, 1964 (cf. illustration 16); (photo: John Goldblatt).
42. *Deep Body Blue*, 1967. Steel painted dark blue, 58½ x 101 x 124 in. Private collection, Boston (photo: John Goldblatt).
43. *Prairie*, 1967 (cf. illustration 29).
44. *Orangerie*, 1969. Steel painted matte pink, 88½ x 64 x 91 in. Collection: Mr Kenneth Noland, New York (photo: John Goldblatt).
45. *Deep North*, 1969–70. Steel, cadmium steel and aluminum, 96 x 228 x 114 in. Collection: Mr Kenneth Noland, New York (photo: John Goldblatt).
46. *Sun Runner*, 1969. Steel painted Rustoleum matte yellow ochre, 72½ x 44 x 100 in. Collection: Mr Guido Goldman, Boston (photo: John Goldblatt).
47. *Sun Feast*, 1969–70. Steel painted yellow, 71½ x 164 x 86 in. Private collection, Boston (photo: John Goldblatt).
48. *Wending Back*, 1969. Steel painted dark grey, 43 x 126 x 102 in. Collection: Cleveland Museum of Art (photo: John Goldblatt).
49. *Georgiana* (first stage), 1969–70. Steel painted dark red, 61 x 115 x 186 in. Collection: Albright Knox Gallery, Buffalo (photo: Guy Martin).
50. *Cadenza*, 1970. Steel painted deep blue, 43 x 43 x 41 in. Collection: Mr and Mrs Arthur Goldberg, New York (photo: John Goldblatt).
51. *Crown*, 1970–71. Steel painted matte pink, 42½ x 82 x 32 in. Collection: David Mirvish Gallery, Toronto (photo: John Goldblatt).
52. *Paul's Turn*, 1971. Rusted steel, 99 x 78 x 59 in. Collection: the artist (photo: Guy Martin).
53. *Side Step*, 1971. Steel and corten steel painted brown, 51 x 115 x 58 in. Collection: Mr Tom Quirk, Melbourne (photo: Guy Martin).
54. *Focus*, in construction, 1971 (U.S. sculpture). Steel rusted and varnished, 46 x 104 x 120 in. Collection: the artist (photo: David Scribner).
55. *Up Front*, 1971 (U.S. sculpture). Steel painted red oxide, 69 x 110 x 46½ in. Collection: David Mirvish Gallery, Toronto (photo: André Emmerich).
56. *Cherry Fair*, 1971. Steel and corten steel painted brown, 36 x 87 x 74 in. Collection: Mr Hanford Yang, New York (photo: André Emmerich).
57. *Straight Cut*, 1972. Steel painted and rusted, 52 x 62 x 51 in. Collection: Lord and Lady Balniel, London (photo: John Goldblatt).
58. *Straight Up*, 1972. Natural and painted steel, 56 x 43 x 68 in. Collection: Mr R. Geddes, Princeton, N.J. (photo: John Goldblatt).
59. *Straight On*, 1972. Steel painted and rusted, 79 x 68 x 52 in. Collection: the artist (photo: John Goldblatt).
60. *Cool Deck*, 1971. Stainless steel, 22 x 64 x 124 in. Private collection. Boston (photo: André Emmerich).
61. *Table Piece CXX*, 1973. Steel varnished, 7 x 63 x 24 in. Collection: the artist (photo: John Goldblatt).
62. *Table Piece CXVI*, 1973. Natural steel, 32 x 25½ x 36 in. Collection: the artist (photo: John Goldblatt).
63. *Straight Run*, 1972. Natural steel, 79 x 137 x 31 in. Collection: Mrs Alan Wurtzburger, Baltimore (photo: John Goldblatt).

Artist's Chronology

1924	Born in London
1946	Studied sculpture at Regent Street Polytechnic
1947–52	Royal Academy Schools
1951–3	Assistant to Henry Moore
1953–66	Taught sculpture two days weekly and later one day weekly at St Martin's School of Art, London
1959	Made first trip to United States.
1960	Made first steel sculptures
1963–4	and Spring 1965 Taught sculpture at Bennington College, Bennington, Vermont, U.S.A.
1968	Renewed regular teaching one day weekly at St Martin's School of Art. Lives in London

One-man exhibitions

1956	Galleria del Naviglio, Milan, Italy
1957	Gimpel Fils, London
1963	Whitechapel Gallery, London
1964	André Emmerich Gallery, New York
1965	Washington Gallery of Modern Art, Washington, D.C. Kasmin Gallery, London
1966	André Emmerich Gallery, New York David Mirvish Gallery, Toronto, Canada Galerie Bischofberger, Zurich, Switzerland
1967	Kasmin Gallery, London Rijksmuseum Kröller-Müller, Otterlo, Holland
1968	André Emmerich Gallery, New York
1969	British Selection, 10th São Paulo Bienal The Arts Council, Hayward Gallery, London
1970	André Emmerich Gallery, New York
1971	David Mirvish Gallery, Toronto Kasmin Gallery, London
1972	André Emmerich Gallery, New York Kasmin Gallery, London
1973	André Emmerich Gallery, New York

Group exhibitions

1955	New Sculptors and Painter–Sculptors, Institute of Contemporary Arts, London 'Contemporary Painting and Sculpture', Leeds City Art Gallery

1957   'New Trends in British Art', Rome/New York Foundation
Arts Council touring exhibitions of sculptures in the open air
'Contemporary British Sculpture', Arts Council exhibition and tours

1958   'Three Young English Artists', 24th Biennale, Venice
'The Religious Theme', Tate Gallery, London
International Exhibition of Sculpture in the open air, Sonsbeek,
    Holland
Pittsburgh International, Carnegie Institute, Pittsburgh,
    Pennsylvania
Contemporary Arts Society exhibition, Tate Gallery, London

1959   Biennial exhibition of open-air sculpture, Carrara, Italy
lère Biennale des Jeunes, Musée National d'Art Moderne, Paris
5th Biennial International Sculpture Exhibition, Middleheim Park,
    Antwerp

1960   Open-air sculpture exhibition, Battersea Park, London
'Contemporary British Sculpture', Arts Council exhibition
Arts Council touring exhibitions of sculptures in the open air

1961   Arts Council touring exhibitions of sculptures in the open air
'Ten Sculptors', Marlborough New London Gallery, London
'New London Situation', Marlborough New London Gallery, London
International Union of Architects Congress, London

1962   'Young English Sculptors', Madrid

1963   Open-air sculpture, Battersea Park, London
'The 118 Show', Kasmin Gallery, London

1964   'Documenta III', Kassel, Germany
'1954–1964, Painting and Sculpture of a Decade', Tate Gallery,
    London
Hampstead artists, Kenwood House, London

1965   'Sculpture from All Directions', World House Galleries, New York
'Seven Sculptors', Institute of Contemporary Art, University of
    Pennsylvania, Philadelphia, Pennsylvania
Kane Memorial Exhibition, Providence, Rhode Island
'British Sculpture of the Sixties', Tate Gallery, London

1966   Open-air Sculpture, Battersea Park, London
Arts Council touring exhibitions of sculptures in the open air
Open-air sculpture, Arnhem, Holland
33rd Biennale, Venice, British Pavilion (Awarded David Bright
    sculpture prize)
'Primary Structures', Jewish Museum, New York

1967   'Color, Image, Form', Detroit Institute of the Arts, International
    Sculpture Exhibition, Guggenheim Museum, New York
'American Sculpture in the Sixties', Los Angeles County Museum,
    Los Angeles, California
'Englische Kunst', Galerie Bischofberger, Zurich, Switzerland
Pittsburgh International, Carnegie Institute, Pittsburgh,
    Pennsylvania

'The 180 Beacon Collection of Contemporary Art', U.S.A.
'Selected Works from the Collection of Mr and Mrs Gates Lloyd',
   Institute of Contemporary Art, University of Pennsylvania,
   Philadelphia, Pennsylvania
'New British Painting and Sculpture', University of California at
   Los Angeles, California

1968 '25 Camden Artists', Camden Arts Festival, London
'Contemporary British Sculpture', Arts Council exhibition and tour
'Noland, Caro, and Morris Louis', Metropolitan Museum of Art,
   New York
Hemis Fair, San Antonio, Texas
'New British Sculpture', Bristol (Open-air and gallery exhibition
   organized by the Arnolfini Gallery)
'Documenta IV', Kassel, Germany
35th Biennale, Venice (central pavilion)

1969 'Stella, Noland, Caro', Dayton's Gallery 12, Minneapolis, Minnesota
'Artists from the Kasmin Gallery', Arts Council Gallery, Belfast,
   Ireland

1970 Leeds City Art Gallery (July)
'British Painting and Sculpture 1960–1970', National Gallery of
   Art, Washington, D.C.
'Contemporary British Art', National Museum of Modern Art,
   Tokyo, Japan
Lincolnshire Association's Gallery, Institute of Contemporary Arts,
   London

1971 Group Show, David Mirvish Gallery, Toronto, Canada
1972 Group Show, Kasmin Gallery, London

Richard Whelan: Anthony Caro

To my parents

Acknowledgements

I want to thank Kermit Champa for the invaluable advice and criticism he gave me while I was writing the Yale senior essay which provided the germ of this book, and for his assistance in my obtaining a grant from Yale which enabled me to travel to London to see the retrospective exhibition of Caro's work at the Hayward Gallery in 1969. I would also like to thank Barbara Reise and Sheldon Nodelman for their useful comments and suggestions. Nikos Stangos and Richard Morphet have been patient and encouraging editors, and I am grateful for their confidence in asking me to write this book. Of course, I must acknowledge my debt to Clement Greenberg and Michael Fried, as must anyone who writes about Caro's work. Many of my ideas have arisen either in agreement with or in reaction against their writings. Caro himself has been generous with his time and information. He has also been a great help in obtaining photographs of the sculpture, as have been the André Emmerich Gallery in New York and the Kasmin Gallery in London.

I especially thank Roberta Smith for her generosity in typing the manuscript and for all her enthusiasm and insights. And finally, I thank my wife, who has taught me much about seeing.

R.W.

We can learn much about the nature of Anthony Caro's art if we consider the nature of the act of welding, which is the crucial technique in the creation of the steel and aluminum sculptures which Caro has been making since 1960. Welding is essentially a process of joining discrete forms together to make a single unit. It is not simply an adhesive process, in which an intermediary substance is introduced to effect the bond; but it is rather a fusile process, which actually intermingles the substances of the parts at the point of juncture.* Caro's sculptures, at their best, embody this particular aspect of welding. They are more than mere constructions; they achieve a quality of spontaneity, a certain inevitability in the profound unity and interdependence of the forms. Caro's working methods foster genuine spontaneity, for he does not make preliminary drawings or maquettes which are then worked up into the finished sculptures: he does not use welding merely as an expedient for joining together pieces of metal into a pre-determined configuration. Instead, each sculpture is evolved completely in terms of the actual raw materials at hand – a varied range of industrial metal forms: boiler tank tops, girders, tubing, propeller blades, and so on. The available vocabulary changes constantly as Caro's instinctive formal responses change. Out of the myriad of available forms the eye at any given moment is pre-disposed, through situation and temperament, to focus on only a very limited set of specific things. Henry Moore has called this unconscious process of selection 'form interest' and has defined his term nicely with an anecdote: 'Sometimes for several years running I have been to the same part of the sea-shore – but each year a new shape of pebble has caught my eye, which the year before, though it was there in hundreds, I never saw. Out of the millions of pebbles passed in walking along the shore, I choose to see with excitement only those which fit in with my existing form interest at the time.'[1] So too with Caro's sculptures, the better the sculpture, the more clearly it bears evidence of Caro's response to qualities in particular forms which weld them together simply through the fact of his simultaneous response to

*Caro himself believes that welding *is* an adhesive process and that this is just what he wanted; that in *making* a sculpture welding is simply that. Physical problems of weight, support, suspension are, to Caro,'what matters. (Ed.)

them. Welding as a physical process is always present as a factor

conditioning that response, for Caro and his welding assistant, Charles
Hendy,* must always work in terms of the empirical possibilities and
limitations of welding. In the course of working, however, they are constantly extending their vocabulary of possibilities, as a dancer who is
continuously strengthening and coordinating his body will, if he learns to
move with his own particular lines of strength, not merely learn to
imitate the movements of others which had previously been beyond his
abilities, but will perform movements which are possible only for him.

Anthony Caro was born in London on 8 March 1924, and spent his
childhood in Farnham, Surrey. He attended Charterhouse public school,
and went on to get his degree in engineering at Christ's College,
Cambridge. After a stint in the Navy at the end of the Second World
War, Caro felt that his childhood interests in drawing and in modelling in clay were important enough to him to warrant further development.[2] Therefore, he enrolled in 1946 at the Regent Street Polytechnic
in London to study sculpture for a year. Then in 1947 he transferred to
the Royal Academy Schools, where he remained until 1952. His
orthodox education provided Caro with technical knowledge and, perhaps
more important, with a formal vocabulary against which he could
later direct his reaction. Nevertheless, although Caro's sculpture departed
radically in the 1960s from the traditional canons of figurative sculpture, there has remained in his art a distinctive quality of disciplined
complexity.

Caro decided in 1950 to ask Henry Moore to give him a job as a
part-time assistant. Moore told him to come back in six months, and so,
when Caro returned six months later, to the day, Moore took him on
as an apprentice. Moore's position as the one British sculptor to gain
international recognition after the Second World War as a great
modern artist posed a problem which was uniquely British, namely that
any young sculptor who wished to escape from the provincialism of
British twentieth-century art without, in a sense, becoming an expatriate,
had to come to terms with Moore's work. As Caro himself said in a
newspaper article in 1960: '[Moore] worked in terms of the mainstream
of avant garde art, and yet his work was intelligible to the English.'[3]
It was just this intelligibility and accessibility that made Moore such a
good teacher for Caro and that made his work so directly important

*Charles Hendy is no longer with Caro. (Ed.)

to young British sculptors. As Caro said, 'All students of sculpture are indebted to him, and all at one time or another in their careers are influenced by his work; he provides an alphabet and a discipline within which to start to develop. His success has created a climate for all us younger sculptors and has given us confidence in ourselves which without his efforts we would not have felt.'[4] Although Moore's success certainly did inspire confidence in young British sculptors simply through the fact that a British sculptor had achieved such great stature in the art world, the increasing acceptability and even expectedness of Moore's art by the early 1950s brought about a gradual rapprochement between Moore and the academy (or, rather, a redefining of the limits of academic style) while, at the same time, Moore seemed to be closing off the very roads he had opened up, because of the depth and exhaustiveness of his exploration of formal motifs and because of the recognizable and distinctive quality of his style. The problem was to learn from Moore without making sculpture that looked like his.

Two characteristics of Moore's art are the primeval, archetypal quality of his sculpture and his carver's handling of materials, a reductive kind of handling which involves great responsiveness to the natural qualities of a particular piece of wood or stone. Caro, in contrast to Moore, had always been a modeller in clay, a material in which both addition and subtraction are possible and which is more anonymous than stone or wood. A sculpture of a standing woman which Caro did in 1951[5] begins to reconcile his modelling with the qualities of primitive art of which Moore was making him aware and looks rather like the prehistoric Venus of Willendorf. The crudeness of the modelling reveals an expressionism alien to Moore, and the ugliness of the figure reflects a temperament unconcerned with Moore's noble articulation of volumes. Dubuffet's 'art brut', and especially his 'Corps de Dames' series, come to mind in looking at Caro's figure.

A similarity to Dubuffet can also be noted in the sculpture done in the 1950s by Eduardo Paolozzi, an exact contemporary of Caro. Paolozzi worked in Paris in 1948–9 and, on his return to London, worked in a style that had its origins in Dada. In the later 1950s he made bronze castings of figures that were constructed from, and encrusted with, small found objects. The sculpture of Caro and Paolozzi differed radically from the English post-war mannerism of Kenneth Armitage, Reg Butler and Lynn Chadwick, all of whom belong to a slightly older generation of sculptors and whose high-strung, tortured and spiny figures with slender tapering limbs owe much to the work done by Moore and Giacometti during the 1940s.

In 1954, the year after he left Moore's studio, Caro made *Man Holding His Foot* [1], a bronze slightly over two feet high. It is a figure of a man with one knee drawn up to his chest, with his shoulders and head pulled forward as he grasps his foot with both hands, and with the other leg extended straight out, somewhat to one side. The crudely featured head is small in proportion to the extremely bulky body, which has massive limbs and a thick, humped back. The heaviness of the figure is offset to some extent by the way in which the roughly modelled surface of the golden-colored bronze catches the light and breaks up its reflection, thus tending to dissolve the mass of the figure.

Man Holding His Foot comes out of a tradition which includes the ancient Greek *Thorn-puller* and Michelangelo's *Crouching Boy*.

1. *Man Holding His Foot*, 1954

Caro's figure differs from the two earlier pieces particularly in its modelling and in its subordination of the look of the body to the feel of the body as experienced from within.[6] Wolffin has said of Michel- angelo's figure: 'The work has the appearance of a solution to a set problem, as though he had really set himself to produce the most complicated figure possible, while removing as little stone and altering the volume of the block as little as possible.'[7] In *Man Holding His Foot*, on the other hand, Caro is concerned with movement and energy rather than with explicitly formal problems. Although most of Caro's figure is drawn up into a cubic space, the extended leg is filled with the energy generated by that compression and thrusts outward from the complexity of the rest of the body into free space, thus breaking out of the space of the carved block in which Michelangelo's figure is con- fined. The *Crouching Boy* reflects Michelangelo's feeling about the body as a prison for the soul, as brute matter to be wrestled with and shaped so that it might become an expression of the soul; the mind of the artist must struggle with his body and with the block of stone. *Man Holding His Foot*, however, reflects a very different attitude to the body, one which sees the body as that which moves and feels and which experiences the world. The mind is the body's response to the world. Since in this view the body becomes very specifically one's own body, which is the sum total of one's limitations, experiences and possibilities, the primary concern is with the body as felt rather than with the body as seen. (I hope it is clear that I am not speaking of any attitudes which Caro may or may not consciously hold, but only of what I *see* in the sculpture.)

The crudeness of the limbs and features of Caro's figure gives *Man Holding His Foot* a primeval quality, a sense of an original exploration of the body, a first groping acquaintance with its extremities, its limita- tions and possibilities. The heaviness of the body expresses the awkward- ness arising from the unfamiliarity of the limbs. The process of discovery depends here on kinesthesia; sight is not important, as the eyes of the man gaze outward without understanding (unlike the eyes of the *Crouching Boy*, which look downward in an effort to grasp the body's action visu- ally). *Man Holding His Foot* resembles, in its forms and in its emphasis on touching and learning, Picasso's *First Steps* (1943) [2]. Caro's figure, however, incorporates the bodies of the mother and child into a single body which expresses the spontaneity of learning and the necessary simultaneity, in terms of one's own body, of the discovery of the possibility of performing a particular action and the actual performance of the action.

The surface modelling of *Man Holding His Foot* explores, in a way that
most cubist sculpture does not, the problem of the ambiguity of the
surface raised in cubist painting. The uneven reflectivity of the polished
bronze tends both to define the surface and to dissolve it optically.
All that we really see of the piece (or of anything) is its surface. Cubist
painting acknowledges that fact and is ultimately more concerned
with the visuality of surface than with the ambiguity of the illusion of
depth, as such. That is to say that cubist painting recognizes the
surface of a painting as the surface of an object which has only surface.
All the interior relationships of a painting must exist on the surface,
where they are accessible to sight. The illusion of depth is just one result
of certain kinds of relationships. The fact that sculpture exists in three
dimensions and occupies space as fully as we do does not make sculpture

2. Picasso, *First Steps*, 1943

inherently any less illusionistic than a painting which uses perspective, especially when we consider that the surface of a sculpture encloses only a hollow space or a block of stone.

The convention of the organic interior of sculpture is as illusionistic as one-point perspective. Sculpture is *seen*, just as painting is *seen*, and just as we project our experience of depth onto a painting which uses perspective or shading, so do we inevitably project our experience of our own bodies on to figural sculpture.

Walter Ong, a theologian who has been concerned with our sensory orientations in different forms of experience, has made some interesting observations on the relationships of sight, touch and sound to exteriors and interiors. He writes: 'Sight presents surfaces (it is keyed to *reflected* light; light coming directly from its source . . . rather dazzles and blinds us) . . . Touch, including kinesthesia, helps form the concepts of exteriority and interiority. We feel ourselves inside our own bodies, and the world as outside . . . But to explore an interior, touch must violate the interior, invade it, even break it open. Kinesthesia, it is true, gives access to my own interior without violation . . . but kinesthesia gives me direct access to nothing but myself. Other interiors are inaccessible to it (except through empathy, indirectly). Sound, on the other hand, reveals the interior without the necessity of physical invasion. Thus we tap a wall to discover where it is hollow inside . . . To discover such things by sight, we should have to open what we examine, making the inside an outside, destroying its interiority as such. Sound reveals interiors because its nature is determined by interior relationships.'[8]

It was to take Caro five years to begin to develop the possibilities which we see in retrospect as germinally present in *Man Holding His Foot*. We might say that these possibilities are present in Caro's piece in much the same way that the germs of Synthetic Cubism and collage are present in Analytical Cubism. As it became clear that the painting was an object that was literally all surface, attention shifted from the analysis of the depicted object to the synthesis of the painting as an object in itself. In collage, that synthesis became a kind of construction which reinforced the ambiguity of the picture plane by pasting paper and other materials onto the surface of canvas and painting over the affixed surface. It was a short, but daring, jump for Picasso from collage through relief to constructed sculpture, in which an object analogous to a painting, but independent of a picture plane, was synthesized in three-dimensional space.

Early in 1959 Caro experimented with such tactics as placing a plaster figure of a woman on a real steel bench, in the hope that the absence

of the usual base would make the experience of the piece more immediate
for the viewer. Then, in the summer of that year, when he was making
plaster sculptures in which he was trying to get away from the image
of the human figure,⁹ Caro met the American critic Clement Greenberg
in London. Greenberg, who had just written an important article on
collage in 1959 and who had long been a great admirer of David Smith's
work, encouraged Caro in his struggle to work out a sculptural style in
which he could express himself fully. Caro's thoughts about non-figurative
sculpture were brought to a climax, and began to realize themselves
during a trip to the United States, made possible by a travel grant, in the
autumn of 1959. Michael Fried says of this visit: 'He spent just over
two months there (and in Mexico) travelling, meeting artists and critics,
looking at pictures and sculptures. In particular he was impressed by

3. *Twenty-four Hours*, 1960

the work of two painters just starting to be recognized, Kenneth Noland and Morris Louis, as well as by the few Pollocks then in New York museums; he saw at least one sculpture by David Smith, whose work he knew from reproductions, and met Smith briefly; and he became friends both with Noland and with the critic Clement Greenberg.'[10]

Upon his return to London, Caro learned how to weld and made a few sculptures in the style of David Smith. In *Twenty-four Hours* [3], done in 1960, Caro finally broke through these experimental works into a style which is completely his own. The piece is composed of three planar forms: a trapezoid which is perpendicular to the ground, on which it rests directly; a disk which seems to float above, behind and to the right of the trapezoid; and a square, inflected slightly away from being parallel to the other two forms. The piece is so frontal that it is almost

4. *Sculpture 2*, 1960

a high relief without any flat background, becoming even more
pictorial, in this respect, than much of David Smith's work.

Smith, who had been a painter before he began making sculpture
and who often made sketches of his ideas for sculptures which were then
translated into metal, made a highly original and richly varied body
of work out of welded metal forms. His work had its roots in Picasso and
Gonzalez's metal sculpture; in Giacometti's early work, such as *Woman
with her Throat Cut* and *The Palace at 4 A.M.*; and in Constructivism, with
its ideal, as Herbert Read puts it, of 'creative engineering'.[11] By the
middle 1950s, the frontality which had always been important in Smith's
work was often combined with the verticality of a standing figure in a
frontal and pictorial image.

One thing which distinguishes *Twenty-four Hours* from both Caro's
bronze figures and his later abstract sculpture is the way in which it is
constructed. The figure's act of touching was crucial in *Man Holding
His Foot*; and we shall see in most of the welded sculpture that the ways
in which forms touch each other are of central importance. The three
main forms in *Twenty-four Hours*, however, do not touch each other, but
are separated and supported by pieces of steel girder, which remain
secondary, structural elements, subordinated to the trapezoid, the disk
and the square. Viewed from some angles, the disk appears to float
in space, completely free of the other forms, denying its all too real means
of support. The three concentric circles on the face of the disk (a band
impressed into the metal, a circle of bolts, and a circle of black paint) give
the disk the air of a target which has been pried away from the square
ground beside it. The construction of the sculpture paraphrases, in a sense,
the traditional split between the support and the medium, the canvas
and the paint, or the structure and the forms.

Twenty-four Hours sits directly on the ground, but in the absence of
the usual intervening pedestal, the trapezoid establishes itself as a
front, base plane, which serves as a foil for the disk and the square, and
as a sort of visual pedestal which is incorporated directly into the
sculpture. Since the trapezoid is a triangle with a small piece cut off near
its apex, the eye tends to complete the triangle, thus giving the sloping
sides of the trapezoid an upward thrust which reinforces the illusory buoyancy of the disk and the square. Because of that support and because
it largely conceals the structural beams, like the screen behind which a
puppeteer stands, the trapezoid acts as a kind of ground for the two
other planes. David Smith had also struggled with the problem of the
base, but reached a solution by making the base part of the structure
of the piece, either as in *The Letter*, where the traditional base and the

framing edge of the metal drawing become clearly integrated, or as
in an untitled sculpture of 1964 [5], where there is no base, as such, but
rather four wheels, which are different enough from both the traditional
base and the rest of the sculpture to take on an active and ambiguous role
in the transition between the work and the ground.

The dark, drab brown color which *Twenty-four Hours* is painted unifies
the sculpture optically and acts as a kind of psychological pedestal,
denoting the piece as something to be looked at. Caro's use of paint, which
has its most important precedent in Smith's work, is analogous in
Twenty-four Hours to Paolozzi's use of bronze casting in the 1950s to give
an ironic respectability to the use of unconventional materials and to
effect an ambiguous transmutation of those materials. The paint, in a
sense, 'casts' the constructed, modelled work into a solid unit.

5. David Smith, Untitled, 1964

In several sculptures of 1960 Caro experimented with various
approaches to frontality and to development in three-dimensional space.
These sculptures each retained at least one upright form which acted
as a reference plane for the other forms. They also continued the split
between planar forms and their constructed supports. *Midday* [6] is
the first sculpture in which Caro transcends the formal problems with
which he was working in *Twenty-four Hours*.

Because of its importance as a truly innovative breakthrough in Caro's
oeuvre, I shall discuss *Midday* in more detail than the later sculptures.
Midday is, in a sense, a foundation for Caro's sculptures of the 1960s, and
I shall base my discussion on the nature of Caro's abstraction, much
of which applies directly to all of the later sculpture.

The first major innovations of *Midday* are its horizontal orientation
and its resultant full three-dimensionality. Caro has, in effect, rotated the
upright reference plane of the earlier sculptures almost ninety degrees
and has thus made the ground the basic reference plane of the work. The
ground is also the reference plane for the movement of our bodies –
standing up, lying down, walking, jumping, and so on. Verticality is
traditionally associated with seeing and with the body as seen.
Horizontality, on the other hand, is associated with movement, duration,
and change, as, for instance, in the context of music.

If we compare *Twenty-four Hours* with *Midday*, we can see how the
visuality of the former yields to the internal physicality of the latter.
The trapezoid of the earlier piece, which was an optical support for the
disk and the square, is replaced in *Midday* by a platform which actually
supports the sections of I-beam. Just as important is the exchange of the
disk, the placement of which creates the illusion that it is floating, for
a section of I-beam which is balanced precariously on one of its small edges.
The logic of the disk is entirely visual; the quality of its effect is determined not so much by the nature of its placement as by the nature of our
vision. In *Midday*, however, there is no such dichotomy of placement
and structure. The size of the section of I-beam and the strength of the weld
determine directly and empirically – through touch and response to
the specific forms – the angle at which the I-beam can be placed. Caro's
background in engineering becomes helpful here, as he begins to
explore the physical possibilities of his material. Since those possibilities
are limited by the force of gravity, the welded steel sculpture assumes
one of the most poignant qualities of the human body in a way in
which stone or bronze figurative sculpture never could. *Midday* has an
internal, physical, expressive logic which is parallel to the logic of
one's own body as it is experienced through kinesthesia. Balance, stress

and inflection are all present perceptively, not merely metaphorically,
in the sculpture.

The interiority and self-ness of *Midday* are assured particularly by the inflection of the long platform away from being parallel to the ground. This inflection acknowledges the ground, but also establishes a reference plane for the sculpture which relates specifically only to the composition of the piece. Reyner Banham has said that '. . . the Brutalists discovered that Form was what you did to Function in making architecture',[12] but Caro seems to have discovered for himself that form and function are mutually determining and that function is nothing more than the internal relationships of the forms to each other. Because of the openness of *Midday*, all its internal relationships are accessible to our sight. But this accessibility of the interior makes our sight function in a

6. *Midday*, 1960

manner ordinarily reserved for hearing – revealing without needing
to penetrate.[13] We must understand clearly that the interior which is
revealed to us in *Midday* is completely different from the kind of
interior which Gonzalez depicts, for instance, in his wrought-iron *Head*
(c. 1935), which seems to endow us with X-ray vision that allows
us to see the brain and the optic nerves. Gonzalez's piece is conceived
simply in terms of literal vision and, as such, portrays the head as
we could know it only by 'violating the interior' of another person's head,
making that interior an exterior. *Midday*, on the other hand, does not
depict an interior; it simply exists as the complex of its interior relationship.
It is, in this sense, like a musical chord, the intricate and rich over-
tones of which are intensified until they congeal into visible form.

Caro paints his sculpture after it has been completely constructed –
after the internal formal relationships have been activated. The
problem of selecting the color of the sculpture then becomes one of
discovering the dominant tone of the formal relationships and
deciding whether to use a color which will put the piece into a major
or minor mode, which will speed up or slow down the rhythm of
the piece, and/or will emphasize the fundamental tone or certain of the
partial tones. (There is also some irony in the color of *Midday*, since
that particular yellow is often used for heavy machinery.) The color
unifies the sculpture optically, isolating it and intensifying the
relationships of the parts to each other and to the whole, while, at the
same time, reflecting and determining the mood of the piece. Wallace
Stevens's words about color in *The Man with the Blue Guitar* could easily
apply to Caro's sculpture: 'The color like a thought that grows out
of a mood . . . half his gesture, half his speech, the dress of his meaning, . . . the weather of his stage, himself.'[14] Since the effect of a
given color on a sculpture is very specific and unpredictable, Caro often
must try several colors in succession before he finds the one that does
what he wants. Although the selection of the color is usually the last step
in making a sculpture, it cannot justifiably be called a secondary prop-
erty, since it represents as important an aesthetic choice as any other in
the piece and, in fact, influences the way we respond to the formal
relationships.

Clement Greenberg, speaking of modern sculpture in general, has said:
'Instead of the illusion of things, we are now offered the illusion of
modalities: namely, that matter is incorporeal, weightless, and exists only
optically like a mirage.'[15] In Caro's work, from *Midday* onwards, it
would be more accurate to speak of the ambiguity, rather than the illusion, of modalities. Indeed, although the sculpture is first perceived

with our eyes, the experience of the work is synesthetic, and our response occurs in the realm of the 'mysterious and profound unity' of Baudelaire's *Correspondances*. The ambiguity of modalities pervades *Midday*, in which the heaviness of the steel and the roughness of the bolts and the welding-torch cuts are contrasted with the delicate balance and the musical, almost elegant, sense of composition that characterize Caro's handling of the forms. Although our understanding of the solidity of the forms is central in our experience of the abstract qualities of heaviness and strength, which are active in the piece, our perception of the sculpture in terms of the resonance of its color and interior relationships inverts Ong's observations and makes the literal sound that results if we tap the surface of the steel a revelation only of the exterior of the piece, while the interior remains accessible only to sight.

In the roughness of its forms and in the personal and direct handling of its material, *Midday* has an abstract expressionist quality, reminiscent particularly of some of Franz Kline's black and white paintings. British artists were exposed to American painting of the 1940s and 1950s in two important shows held at the Tate Gallery in 1956 and 1959. The British painting which was directly influenced, at least at first, by abstract expressionism, tempered the American style with the characteristically British traits of concern for technical skill, gracefulness, complexity of internal relationships, and ambiguity, all of which are also reflected, to some extent, in *Midday*. If we compare *Midday* with an untitled piece [5] of 1964 in which David Smith also uses sections of I-beams, we can see that the differences between Caro and Smith have less to do with specifically English and American sensibilities than with the individual temperaments of the two sculptors. Smith's sculpture is no more expressionistic or less complex than Caro's. Smith arranged his forms vertically, like a standing figure, but the rectangularity of the piece creates several alternative frontal views, which give the piece pictorial complexity and ambiguity. The balanced right-angle beam represents the same kind of expressive gesture that the balanced I-beam in *Midday* represents, but the effects are very different in the two sculptures, especially since the position of Smith's L-shaped beam is the only inflection away from strict rectangularity in the piece and since Smith's piece alludes to the configuration of the human body. Smith's evident involvement with the human figure relates his work, more than *Midday*, to the mainstream of modern European sculpture. (It is interesting to note that two sculptures by Caro were included in the exhibition of American Sculpture in the Sixties, held at the Los Angeles County Museum of Art in 1967.)

The American artist who, besides David Smith, had the most direct and important influence on Caro is the painter Kenneth Noland. Michael Fried has said of Caro and Noland: 'If the central concept for understanding Caro's art is that of the body, the central concept for understanding Noland's is that of personal identity, of the self.'[16] I would suggest, however, that what Caro and Noland have in common is precisely that their art is based on the unity of the body and the self. In discussing *Twenty-four Hours* I said that the planar forms and the structure which supported them remained separate from each other. In *Midday*, however, the forms themselves are the structure, and the structure the forms. Form is not imposed, but responded to and integrated. Caro does not make any working drawings or models, but rather he works directly with the pieces of metal which are always scattered in piles around his studio. His approach is pragmatic, as he tries various combinations of metal pieces, often building a sculpture up and making it quite complex and then paring it down and simplifying it. In an interview with Andrew Forge, Caro has said of the process of making a sculpture: 'This whole operation for me doesn't come out of a concept in the mind, it comes out of some vague idea, plus the stuff.' Forge: 'The actual stuff?' Caro: 'Yes, the presence of the stuff. You have to lift it and put it here and that leads you to do the other things, just as a painter is influenced by the viscosity of paint.'[17] The technique of staining which Kenneth Noland uses in his paintings achieves an analogous integration of idea and materials. In his paintings of the last several years, part of the canvas is almost always left exposed, and the weave of the fabric shows clearly through the stained color, relieving the canvas largely of its traditional role of support and making it an active part of the painting, as color and surface. The nature of the paint is also important, since Noland's acrylic stains are different in nature from Morris Louis's magna stains, or Helen Frankenthaler's oil stains or Jackson Pollock's Duco stains. The clear and distinct stripes, chevrons, and concentric circles of color in Noland's paintings create a sharp rhythm that is very different from the glissando of Morris Louis's paintings, for example.

John Russell has said of Caro: 'He takes pieces of metal that in themselves are inert, anonymous, inexpressive . . . These pieces he treats as Matisse treated individual colors: in the belief, that is to say, that none of them is beautiful in itself, but that all can become beautiful in their relation to others. Singly, they are nothing; put together, they turn out to have an extraordinary natural eloquence.'[18] Caro and Noland both owe much to Matisse's late paper cut-outs, especially those in the book *Jazz*. Matisse fully realized in *Jazz* the musical and improvisatory

nature of his cut-outs and the expressive potential of relationships of
simple colored forms. It was as if, after having explored the possibilities offered by the masks and sculpture of Africa, Matisse recognized
the inseparability of the visual arts from dance and music in traditional African culture; the rhythm of the music contained in essence
the movements of the body and its hopes and fears. Matisse discovered that combinations of intensely colored, closely valued simple
forms could express visually the rhythm and inflections of jazz. His
forms, however, always remained, if not representational, then at least,
organic. Noland has refined Matisse's rhythmic handling of color so
that shape becomes less tangible (in the targets) and later (in the horizontal stripes) becomes relative area, a function of intensity and
duration which directly affects the quality of the color. As we have said,

7. *Sculpture Seven,* 1961

Caro's color works primarily as the tone, timbre or mood of the inter-relationships of the forms, which can articulate rhythms as complex or as subtle as those created by Matisse's colored forms or Noland's bands of color.

In *Sculpture Seven* (1961) [7], Caro tried to enlarge the role of color in his sculpture by painting the piece three colors. Three large I-beams are painted a glossy medium green; one small I-beam is painted a rich chocolate brown; and an even smaller T-beam is painted an intense, matte, cobalt blue. Like *Twenty-four Hours* [3], *Sculpture Seven* invites an essentially frontal and pictorial reading. In fact, the sculpture seems to transliterate the effect of staining raw canvas into the language of steel girders. The two large rear beams build a wall that works like the canvas. The brown beam penetrates that wall and both wedges the fabric of that 'canvas' apart and projects from that background. The large green beam in front acts like the areas of raw canvas that themselves become color and both identify with, and stand out from, the background of the canvas. Unfortunately (whether Caro actually conceived the sculpture in these terms or not), this arrangement of forms appears rather contrived, and the color only emphasizes the fragmentation of the forms. The interrelationships of the forms are somehow too forced and studied, making the sculpture seem brittle and keeping it from the feeling of repose charged with subtle tensions that it almost achieves.

The horizontal disposition of forms is more successful in *Sculpture Two* (1962) [8], an open and playful composition that moves exuberantly along the plane of the ground. The green which the whole piece is painted unites the forms over the rambling expanse of the work. Although the forms seem at first to sprawl out in a staccato, impromptu dance, that dance becomes more visibly measured as we perceive the way in which forms echo each other within the piece. We tend at first to read the piece (in the view in the photograph) from left to right and then to get into its central orientation. The beam which lies directly on the ground estab-lishes the horizontal plane of the ground, and the beam perpendicular to it defines the vertical. The inflection of the beam on the far left away from the vertical is echoed clearly by the inflection of the beam on the far right away from the horizontal. In between these two beams, which establish an orientation within the sculpture which is alternative to, and as valid as, the orientation established by the ground, there is a play of inflection and perpendicularity, relative to the ground and to the two beams, punctuated by two narrow beams that seem to alight at irra-tional angles on the sturdier beams and a section of I-beam and a piece of bent angle iron that are like splashes of bright color in the com-

position. The curve of the angle iron especially rebuffs the rectangularity
of the rest of the forms and suggests the kind of warping which results
from the ambiguous perpendicularity and parallelism of the beams. Although
the beams are far more dispersed than the beams in *Sculpture Seven*,
the piece is unified by its active three-dimensional development, its internal
logic, and its elemental energy of breadth and movement.

   Sculpture Two, like many of Caro's best sculptures, is characterized by
complex inflections against an open, but relatively rigid, framework
(here, the beam on the ground and the beam perpendicular to it), which
establishes or paraphrases the plane of the ground within the piece.
Early One Morning [11A, B], *Titan* [15], *Trefoil* [34], and *After Summer*
[36A, B] all have a beam, a plane, or a framework that runs along
the ground, or is parallel to it, around which the other forms are developed.

8. *Sculpture Two*, 1962 (cf. illustration 39)

These central forms give their respective sculptures a gravity that is
both literal and metaphorical: literal, because they articulate the ground;
metaphorical, because they create a sense of immutability in contrast
with which the subtleties of placement and inflection assume a tremendously increased significance and impact. The mechanism of the
framework and the inflections against it work like the structure of wit:
a spontaneous remark transforms its context and forces us to see that
context in a new and momentarily disorienting way. (Its active formal
role distinguishes this kind of framework from the merely structural
framework of *Twenty-four Hours*.)

Caro's use of forms to define the ground and then to challenge and
transform it might be said to parallel his enduring involvement with, and
reactions against, academic art, as well as his use of the modern
artistic tradition as a kind of ground on which to work. Caro's relationship to the modern tradition, as a result of his teaching and his being
a European artist who became very involved in post-war American art,
resembles that of Hans Hofmann, who was a great teacher and an
important figure in American abstract expressionist painting. Hofmann
often spoke of two forces – roughly equivalent to Nietzsche's Apollonian and Dionysiac – as present and active in his work.[19] The Apollonian
is plastic and rational, involving the lessons learned from the artists
of the past about color, form, structure, and composition; the Dionysiac
is musical, irrational and spontaneous. And yet, if we are to respond
to either Hofmann's or Caro's art, we must recognize that the Apollonian
and the Dionysiac became reconciled, mutually dependent, and completely interrelated aspects of a single unity in the shifting ground, the
continuum, of the work. The Apollonian without the Dionysiac would
be mute form; the Dionysiac without the Apollonian would be formless.
Like the yin and yang of Chinese philosophy, the traditional and the
spontaneous, the context and the gesture are inseparable. The formal
vocabularies change, and even become different languages, entailing
new specific problems and possibilities, but the changes are all contained
within the fundamental, transcendent act of making art. We suggested
at the beginning of this essay that Caro's technique of making sculpture
reflects the way in which he responds to artistic tradition. He cuts and
welds together the things he responds to most intensely, uniting them
tangibly as they are united in the fact of his response. We might
apply John Hersey's definition of genius to Caro: 'True genius arranges
old material in a way never seen before'.

Caro's sculpture is particularly distinguished by the richness of his
imagination. It is always amazing to see how different each sculpture looks

from the others. The jump from one sculpture to the next will take a
direction as unexpected and unpredictable as the direction of Caro's responses. After *Sculpture Two*, Caro tried to make a sculpture which
wasn't so solid and tangible. He turned to aluminum tubing as a material
which was strong and light, something which could be manipulated
more easily than steel into the kind of configurations that he had experimented with in his placement of the narrow beams in *Sculpture Two*.
Hopscotch [9], a sculpture constructed entirely of aluminum, sparkles with
the immanence of movement. The material, once Caro began to work
with it and to explore it, seems to have revealed unanticipated possibilities
for construction which is at once delicate and strong. The construc-
tivist ideal of creative engineering comes into play in the labyrinthine
structure of the piece, but we lose all idea of structure as a separate

9. *Hopscotch*, 1962

quality and get a feeling of the suspension of lines and planes in space
by their own energy as interacting vectors. The whole space in and
around the sculpture is charged with a shifting, directional energy that
holds the sculpture together. Long horizontal tubes, which seem to
float in space, provide a visual framework, like the diagram of the game
from which the title is taken, for the short flat pieces which jump,
and for the longer, corrugated sections, which leap through the sculpture
and which, at the same time, both support and are supported by the
tubular framework.

Hopscotch is the first of the very few large sculptures which Caro has
not painted. The exposed surface of the metal works rather like the
surface of the bronze in *Man Holding His Foot* [1]; it both defines and
dissolves the forms. A certain tension inherent in the material is

10. *Sculpture Three*, 1962

betrayed by the reflective, but slightly dull, surface of the metal. Since the qualities of the metal all give the sculpture its distinctive character, and since the configuration of the sculpture emphasizes those qualities, it is natural that Caro should choose to let the color of the metal itself set the rhythm of the work.

Although there are, in retrospect, hints throughout Caro's work of 1962 of the incubation of *Early One Morning* [11A, B], the actual work catches us unprepared. *Sculpture Two* [8] introduces extensive development along the plane of the ground and juxtaposition of rectilinear and curving forms. *Sculpture Three* [10] returns to the trapezoid motif of *Twenty-four Hours* [3] and projects, nearly parallel to the ground and about seven feet above it, a long straight, thin beam along which are arranged curving, wrought-iron-like forms which rest on the beam or

11A. *Early One Morning*, 1962

which hang from it as much as they support it. But, even though the roots of the formal organization of the sculpture go clearly back as far as *Midday*, *Early One Morning* is an extraordinary and spontaneous work. It certainly illustrates Baudelaire's maxim, *'Le beau est toujours bizarre'*.

Early One Morning is a very large sculpture, just over twenty feet long, made of steel and aluminum and painted bright vermilion. Seen straight on [11B], the piece becomes flattened out and resembles some of Kandinsky's paintings of the early 1920s or a collage mounted on the plane of the rear rectangle. The tensions of expansion into space are introduced in the frontal view of the piece as the foremost forms, particularly the large cross, extend visually far beyond the limits of the rear rectangle. The juxtaposition of rectangular sections of I-beam and pieces of vaguely

11B. *Early One Morning*

organic, bent aluminum tubing creates a formal tension within the work which begins to be resolved in the cross in which the two kinds of forms literally come closer together and approach each other formally, as the steel crosspiece is more slender and linear than the I-beams, and the tubing straightens out and becomes thicker.

As one moves around to the side of the sculpture, the tremendous spatial depth between the front cross and the rear rectangle becomes apparent. The whole piece opens up to release the forms from the compression and ambiguous shallowness of the frontal view to reveal a large sector of defined, but empty, space at the rear of the piece. The movement into depth is bisected by the two sections of I-beam which flank the long horizontal bar. The channel of the narrower beam runs vertically, and the channel of the wider beam, which is almost as wide as the narrow beam is high, is rotated ninety degrees to run horizontally, creating a kind of transitional vortex between the linear and planar elements, as the beams themselves are partly linear and directional and partly planar. They also serve to solidly anchor the piece, which otherwise touches the ground only with thin tubes. The strength of the beams is necessary to close off the space defined by the rear planes, space which had, from the front viewpoint, visually contained the linear elements and which is now emptied, leaving a great, charged vacuum. The two horizontal planes levitate, as if they were being sucked up by the vacuum. They seem to be pressed against the long spine of the sculpture by a force trying to enter the charged space from below. The linear elements press into the space even from behind, as the configuration of the pieces which support the rear rectangle is rendered visible by the pattern of the bolts which connect the pieces. The color acts strongly to unite the linear and planar forms visually across the expanse of the piece and to subsume them into the totality of the sculpture. The intensity and sharpness of the color echo the staccato quality of the placement of the forms.

Sculpture has traditionally expanded vertically, the only direction in which it could expand without expanding beyond the confines of the pedestal. (Giovanni da Bologna's *Rape of the Sabine Woman* is the classic illustration of this tendency.) Since people ordinarily do not move vertically, they were forced to look up at the work, which remained at a distance. Caro, however, intends us to get up close to his sculpture and to become involved in the interrelationships of the parts. Because his sculptures generally expand horizontally, we can be more or less equally close to all the parts of the work as we walk around it. Caro said in an interview in 1961: 'I prefer to think of my sculptures indoors. Indoors they should expand into space. Outside, when you get back to look at them from a distance, the grip of the sculpture is diffused.'[20] Caro constructed *Early One Morning* in the very small space of his garage. (The front end extended right out through the door.) Therefore, when the sculpture is displayed in an open space outside, our reaction to it as a gestalt is at odds with Caro's intentions. To come upon one of Caro's sculptures in a landscape is an almost surrealist experience, like seeing one of Magritte's matter-of-fact representations of extraordinary and inexplicable phenomena occurring in otherwise ordinary environments, but, since Caro is not at all concerned with what is probable or improbable in terms of the relation of the piece to its setting, but rather only with what is possible within the sculpture itself, that experience is quite irrelevant and distracting. Unfortunately, most of Caro's pieces

12. *Pompadour*, 1963

cannot be photographed as they are meant to be seen. In order to
show the whole sculpture, the photographer must stand too far away,
and to enable the photographer to stand back, inevitably, we lose all
sense of the intimacy of the work that we feel when we are close to it.

Pompadour (1963) [12] is a sculpture made of aluminum sheets, beams,
strips, and tubing, painted a rich pink, which develops the motif of the
upright plane in *Early One Morning* into an elaborate dance of six planes.
The elegant curving strips connect the planes into three pairs, like
couples in a dance, and the beams provide an axis of movement for
each couple. The progression from left to right is like the sequence of
movements in a concerto by Mozart, who is one of Caro's favorite
composers: allegro, adagio, allegro. The pair of planes at the left performs
a sweeping, dramatic movement, with one plane rotated and set on the
ground at an angle. Its beam is inflected slightly away from the vertical
established by the beam of the center pair, which is more restrained in
its subtle movement back into space. The beam on the right is tilted sharply
and directs the movement of the forward plane up and to the right of
the rear plane, to which it is connected by a strip which arcs downward
and to the side. Pieces of thin, flat tubing support the planes and connect the sections of the piece, which are also connected visually by the
strong motif of the planes. As in *Hopscotch*, the lightness of the aluminum enables Caro to create a feeling of buoyancy. The color, Rose Pompadour, sets the key of the composition and gives the sculpture its title.

In *Month of May* (1963) [13], an exuberant, open and linear sculpture,
Caro uses three colors to distinguish the different formal elements and
to complement the rhythm of their interplay. Two squat sections of I-beam
and two long, thin bars are painted an intense magenta; the thin,
angular pieces of tubing are painted slightly ochre orange; and a single
long piece of thick, curving tubing is painted a deep yellowish green.
The success of the polychrome in this work depends largely on its active
formal role. Just as the curving tube breaks through the tangle of tensions of the ground-hugging I-beams, the diagonal bars, and the multidirectional, but primarily vertical, thin tubes into a twisting, inexor-
able upward surge, so does the green resolve in itself the tensions between
the magenta and the orange. The intense magenta, which covers more
unbroken surface than the other two colors, is only partly balanced by the
orange. By leaning toward yellow and by asserting itself strongly
through its distinctive form, the green works with the orange to balance
the magenta.

Because of its openness and its concern with tension and balance,
Month of May might be compared with Alexander Calder's mobiles, which

are, however, more explicitly organic in their forms and movement
than is Caro's sculpture. Caro creates a configuration of fixed forms that
is experienced as rhythm when one is close to the sculpture, and Calder
creates a system within which there is an infinite number of possible configurations, the particular configurations which one sees being determined by chance. Since Caro's primary concern remains with the specific
angles at which specific forms are placed to each other, his work has
little to do with the chance arrangements of moving, geometric or organic
forms that characterize Calder's work.

In the autumn of 1963, a retrospective exhibition of Caro's early
abstract sculpture was held at the Whitechapel Gallery in London, more
or less marking the end of the first phase of Caro's development. At
the same time, Caro went to the United States to teach at Bennington

13. *Month of May,* 1963

College in Vermont for a year. Kenneth Noland and Jules Olitski were both
at Bennington, and David Smith's house at Bolton Landing, New York,
was not very far away. In this atmosphere, in the winter and spring of
1964, Caro made a series of sculptures, using a single, distinctive form
as their shared motif. We have seen how Caro had used I-beams and
aluminum tubing, separately and together, in most of his sculptures,
often carrying a motif such as upright planes from one piece to another,
but we have not seen Caro take a single form – in this case a manu-
factured piece of steel in the shape of a letter Z with right angles – and
improvise a series of variations (seven in all) on that theme. This is an
instance where Caro responded clearly to a specific form and its qualities
of balance, openness, and multidirectionality – qualities with which he
had been working in his sculptures and which he now found concentrated

14. *Flats*, 1964

in a single form – and then explored and developed the possibilities of that form. *Flats* [14], the second sculpture of the series, has two identical units, placed parallel to each other on the ground, each unit made of two Zs welded together so that two faces are joined completely; two faces are tangent; and two faces are parallel. The two units, which are painted fire-engine red, are connected along their central corresponding edges by a ten-foot long piece of narrow angle iron painted royal blue. A shorter piece of angle iron connects corresponding points on the top edges of the two parallel faces of each unit. These strips, which are parallel to each other, are united to the first strip of angle iron by their color and form but do not actually touch that first piece.

In *Flats* Caro does not simply explore the relationships between two identical, rather complex asymmetrical forms placed next to each other. Instead, he imposes a grid of angle iron which variously connects the forms, emphasizes their parallelism, concentrates and extends their axes, and, in the case of the two parallel strips, divides the whole piece into three sections – the left outside, the right outside, and the inside, which becomes an almost independent configuration with status equal to the two forms, a configuration like the lines of force between the opposite poles of two bar magnets. The two units are neither separate, for each is tied to the other by form and color and the fact of their interaction (either form alone would be very different from what it is with the other form beside it), nor identical, since the presence of each form changes the other in a way that is different from the way itself is changed (one form has a form on its right, the other on its left), and since the asymmetry of each form creates an asymmetry in the whole sculpture, just as when two bar magnets come together by attraction to form one bar, one end remains the north pole and the other end the south.

Titan [15], a classically ordered and restrained sculpture (the sixth in the series with Z forms), continues the exploration of the relationships of forms placed near each other on the ground. The wall, which is only about one foot high, moves along the ground and articulates the ground more clearly than any form in Caro's earlier work. The swastika-like forms inside the quadrant defined by the wall and the I-beam outside it are both leaned against the wall, which simultaneously both connects and separates them and also merges the planar and multidirectional qualities of the swastika-like form with the solidity and simplicity of the I-beam. The forms are unified into a single, isolated, complex phenomenon by the deep blue color, leaning slightly toward purple, which the whole sculpture is painted. It is rather difficult to understand why *Titan* was included in the much-discussed Primary Structures show at

the Jewish Museum in New York in 1966, especially when the success of
the sculpture depends entirely on precisely the kind of interior relationships that most so-called Minimal sculptors seek to eliminate from their
work.

In *Bennington* [16] Caro continues to use a wall, but temporarily leaves
the motif of the Z-shaped forms, instead leaning three identical sections
of I-beam against one arm of the T-shaped wall. The symmetry of the
I-beams creates a very different relationship among them than exists
between the forms in *Flats* or *Titan*. We are reminded at first of one of
Donald Judd's wall-pieces in which four identical metal cubes, evenly
spaced, are connected by a hollow, square, aluminum tube. The aims of
the two sculptors, however, are very different. Judd has said: 'it isn't
necessary for a work to have a lot of things to look at, to compare, to

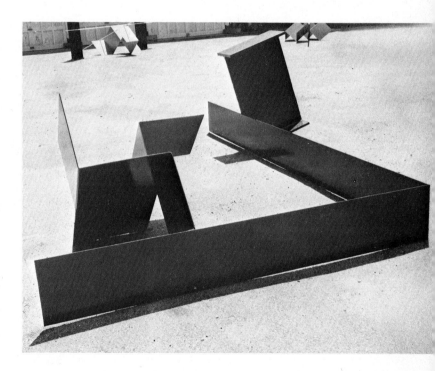

15. *Titan*, 1964 (cf. illustration 40)

analyze one by one, to contemplate. The thing as a whole, its quality
as a whole, is what is interesting.'[21] To continue the metaphor of sound.
Judd's work is involved not so much with rhythm as with the rever-
berations of a single note that is isolated by its timbre and clarity from
ordinary sounds. Although *Bennington* is so open that we cannot help
getting an impression of it as a whole, that first impression is clarified as
we see and respond to the grayness in its dark blue color, the slightly
raised elevation of one arm of the wall, the play of the symmetrical arrangement of the I-beams against the asymmetry of the whole sculpture, and
the angle at which the I-beams are leaned against the wall (that
angle working, like the angles in the illustrations attributed to Takayoshi
of *The Tale of Genji*, to create a definite mood, here one, perhaps, of quiet
expectation).

16. *Bennington*, 1964 (cf. illustration 41)

In *Wide* [17], a sculpture done after his return to London, Caro
drastically shortened the wall and made it a foil for three pieces of flat
aluminum tubing that fan upward and forward from a single point
on its lower edge. The center piece of tubing is slightly larger than the
other two. This difference of size and the differences of the angles of
the tubing in relation to the wall distinguish this group of three forms
from the three I-beams in *Bennington*, with which *Wide* seems to be
engaged in a kind of dialogue. A single piece of angle iron rests on the
upper edge of the wall and extends forward with a long, gentle, downward shape until it touches the ground, when it angles upward to echo
the movement of the three pieces of tubing. The movement of this
angle iron is somewhat analogous to the change in elevation in the long
arm of the wall in *Bennington*. The bright crimson color of the sculp-

17. *Wide*, 1964

ture gives the thin, linear forms a more resonant volume and amplifies
the expansive energy of this refined piece.

When Caro returned to Bennington in the spring of 1965, he made
one last sculpture with the Z-shaped forms. *Shaftsbury* [18] is a
more romantic work that *Titan*; its rich purple lake color sets the mood
for the complexities of the piece, in which one arm of the wall forms
about a seventy-five degree angle with the ground, carrying its attached
Z with it and mimicking the angle of the I-beam. The configuration
of the wall echoes roughly both the Z and the I shapes of its neighboring
forms.

In an interview in 1961 Caro said: 'There's a fine-art quality about
European art, even when it's made from junk. America made me see that
there are no barriers and no regulations . . . There's a tremendous

18. *Shaftsbury*, 1965

freedom in knowing that your only limitations in a sculpture or painting are whether it carries its intentions or not, not whether it's
"Art".'[22] In a sculpture like *Smoulder* [19] Caro reacts to the openness
and directness he feels in America. He cuts away all the fat and gets
down to the bones of his sculpture, where every subtle variation of form
or placement is completely exposed. *Smoulder* might be said to be the
most basic skeleton of *Shaftsbury*, an observation which is reinforced by
the fact that the two sculptures are painted exactly the same color.
The solid cylinder of *Smoulder* might be said to correspond to the tilted
wall with its Z-form in *Shaftsbury*; the angle between the cylinder and
the flat bar is almost the same as the corresponding angle in the earlier
piece; and the angle between the bar and the vertical channel beam
exaggerates the rise in the elevation of the third section of the wall in

19. *Smoulder*, 1965

Shaftsbury and, at the same time, echoes the form and the essential
verticality of the I-beam. The relationships between the cylinder, the bar,
and the channel beam and the angles at which they are placed concentrate the complexities of *Shaftsbury* into a completely independent
masterpiece that represents the essence of Caro's sculpture.

If we say that *Smoulder* is the distillate of the still-life aspect of Caro's
work, then we might say that *Eyelit* [20] is the distillate of the engineered
aspect of his work, which we saw being developed particularly in
Hopscotch. *Eyelit*, which is painted a cerulean blue, consists simply of a
long, thin angle which appears to project downward at a sharp diagonal to touch very gently a short, thick, solid cylinder which rests on two
tiny flat strips on the ground. The piece seems to mock the idea of
structure as a separate problem and to remain nonchalant in the pre-

20. *Eyelit*, 1965

cision of its balance, as if we should know instinctively that a sculpture so meticulously proportioned in its extraordinary symmetry must naturally achieve literal balance.

Slow Movement [21], done after Caro's return to London, depends on silhouette more than any other sculpture since *Twenty-four Hours*. The central form of *Slow Movement* is, in fact, like a refined, elongated version of the trapezoid in that earlier sculpture. Two of the shapes in *Slow Movement* were cut out from a sheet of steel, as none of Caro's shapes had been since the rough, cut-out trapezoid in *Twenty-four Hours*. The steep incline of the sides leads the eye, even more than in *Twenty-four Hours*, to continue upwards and to complete the triangle, thus increasing the perceived height of this four-foot-high sculpture. The shape on the left resembles the central shape placed on its side, but its right

21. *Slow Movement*, 1965

angle and its more completely triangular shape create many subtle tensions between the two forms. The angle iron on the right stabilizes and continues the horizontal movement of the left-hand shape, to which it is nearly parallel, paraphrasing the illusory vertical extension of the central shape. When the horizontal and forward movement of this extension is transmitted through the base of the central shape and across the space dominated by the vertical movement of that shape, there occurs a curious warping of the central shape and the space around it. The thin, linear angle iron has such power that it somehow transforms the right-hand edge of the tall trapezoid and makes it work more as a discrete line than as an edge. Moving to the left across the even, dark blue surface of the shape, we can sense a modulation that is not too different in effect from that which Olitski achieves through his sprayed

58

22. *Strip*, 1965

surfaces with thin lines along one corner in his paintings of the last few years. We become aware of the central shape both as a plane and as a silhouette. The left-hand edge in the photograph asserts itself fully as an edge both of the solid form and of the tilted, receding plane of space defined by that edge and the adjacent edge of the left-hand form.

The proportions of *Strip* [22] are quite extraordinary. The sculpture is seven inches high and six and a half feet long. A relatively heavy aluminum girder, about five feet long, connects a thin, inverted V-shaped form and a small rectangular block with a triangle attached to it. The more the girder seems to separate the end forms, the more the tension between the forms increases. It is as if the two forms were stretching a piece of elastic between them, and the farther apart they move, the more forcibly they are pulled together. The smallness of the sculpture and its

23. *Away,* 1966

bright red color compress and concentrate the energy of this struggle of solid and open forms, right and acute angles, and relative weights.

Having learned much from his American works about the essential nature of his sculpture, Caro could return with renewed understanding and imagination to making sculptures with many parts. The tension of *Strip* becomes elaborated into a highly complex circuit of vectors in *Away* [23], done in 1966. The sheet of corrugated steel is a force which winds through space, dividing and beginning to enclose, but always moving forward with controlled power. Its great force is channelled into the long, straight, low plane, which directs and intensifies the force. The two sections of channel beam are a dense, restraining barrier through which the vector penetrates and beyond which momentum keeps it moving. The edges of these beams point in the direction of movement, registering their reactions as forces to the superior force of the planar vector.

The long bar parallel to this movement restates the force, direction, and unity of the movement. The two upright angle irons that support the bar are placed considerably off to one side of the bar's center of gravity, making the bar extend, as if through momentum, farther toward the direction of the movement of the whole sculpture. The positioning of the bar on the two uprights sets up a balanced circuit of tensions in those uprights, as one is understood to push up, while the other pulls down, making the two identical forms into opposing vectors. The asymmetry of the linear configuration, which is heaviest at the far end of the sculpture, balances the asymmetry of the planar configuration, the heaviest part of which is the corrugated form. The dark blue color helps to make the unity of the sculpture more immediately apparent and adds an element of restraint to the almost excessively dynamic sculpture.

Red Splash [24] deals with reality and illusion and with the perception of depth in space. When seen from one particular position, the four unequal posts of the sculpture appear as if they might be four equal posts in a perspectival representation of deep space, but the posts, the tallest of which is just under four feet high, are actually placed only a few feet apart. The posts diagonally opposite each other are connected by strips of wire mesh, one strip about three times as wide as the other, which knit the posts together visually and which also serve as a kind of shifting grid to emphasize the ambiguous sizes of the posts.

As one walks around the sculpture, the posts do not, of course, change in relative size, as they should to maintain the perspectival illusion of depth. The ambiguous illusion of posts of equal size seen in depth yields to a sense of bizarre distortion. When one stands near the two short

posts, one gets a feeling which is like looking out from the distance toward
the front plane in a painting in which everything but one's own body
is in perspective. The mesh, however, still retains its constant grid, thus
warping the sense of perspective even farther, while the solid rectangle
attests the substantiality of the mesh which supports it. In experiencing
the piece, one is first shown the illusion of an illusion; then one is
made to see the distortion of that illusion; and finally one is forced to
recognize the simple reality of the formal statement. The intense red
color of *Red Splash* energizes the space around the sculpture and expands
its relatively small forms. Through its ebullient brightness the color
also adds to the playful spirit of the ironic logic of the sculpture.

Carriage [25], a blue-green sculpture done in 1966, is related in many
ways to *Early One Morning* [11A, B], in which Caro developed a frontal,

24. *Red Splash*, 1966

pictorial situation which was contrasted with the experience of depth and
the attraction of forms across space which were presented by the side
view of the sculpture. The three upright bars and two horizontal cross-
bars of *Carriage* relate to each other strongly across space and seem,
from one viewpoint, to become aligned into a flat, frontal composition.
The tall, front upright and the rear crossbar come together visually
to form an ambiguous cross which echoes on a large scale the small,
real cross in front. The inflections away from the planes defined by
the sections of mesh, themselves not parallel to each other, create a complex series of variations on a theme of movement in depth within an
ambiguous spatial framework.

As one moves around the sculpture, the relationships of the parts that
have been stated from the frontal viewpoint remain very active. (In

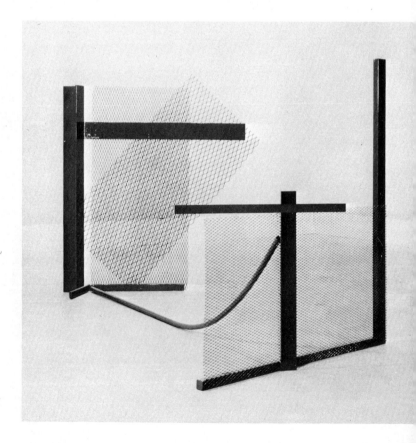

25. *Carriage*, 1966

this respect and in its wit and controlled order, *Carriage* is reminiscent of Bach's Goldberg Variations.) The rear crossbar seems so related to the front upright that even when the sculpture is seen from the side, there is an extraordinary tension across the space between the two parts. Since the tubing is all that literally connects the two sections of the sculpture, and since it also makes their separation explicit and defines the distance between them, the tubing serves to channel and to control the great energy that is transmitted among the forms. The graceful and relaxed curve of the tubing belies the almost electrical energy with which it and the space through which it passes are charged.

Although, as we have noted, Caro's formal imagination is tremendously rich, there is always, as in any artist's work, the danger of becoming caught in a personal mannerism, where the work begins to

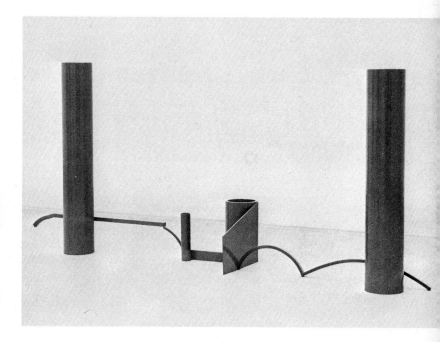

26. *Horizon*, 1966

play too much within the limited scope of its own conventions. In
Horizon [26], which is painted a light, slightly pinkish brown, Caro
seems to have taken his forms too much for granted and to have
become too blatantly involved in composition, in insistently balancing
the asymmetrical arrangement of forms within the symmetry of
the two large uprights. The logically deduced structure of the sculpture is simply not convincing. *Span* [27] begins to avoid a similar
predicament through its sheer exuberance and its three-dimensional
movement (punctuated by the two diagonals, the punning relationship of the grid and the open rectangle, and the dead-pan expressiveness
of the cylinder on the ground) but succumbs ultimately to the
rigidity imposed on it by the obtrusive cut-out forms around which
it is organized.

27. *Span*, 1966

The Window [28] marks a turning away from the particular kind
of horizontally developing connection of forms which evolved
from *Sculpture Two* [8], and which had lost much of its conviction
and freshness by 1966. The new direction in Caro's sculpture is
first stated clearly in *Red Splash* [24], the central orientation and full
round organization of which defines and changes a volume of
space and escapes from the kind of balance epitomized (and almost
exhausted) by *Strip* [22]. *Carriage* begins to shape a space, but it
still operates with the tension created by two similar elements which
are separated and connected by a third, dissimilar element. *The
Window*, however, moves around the edges of a space, embracing it and
filling it with energy, without actually penetrating it. The configurations centering on the mesh and the solid planes are connected by a

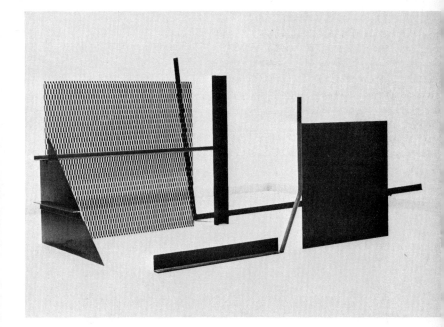

28. *The Window*, 1966–7

piece of angle iron which becomes, itself, a third, equal element, which outlines two edges of a square plane of space (in conversation with the solid plane and the solid-open plane of the mesh) and then, like the line across the mesh and the bar on the ground adjacent to the solid plane, extends linearly beyond the plane. The use of two colors – a dark industrial green and an olive green – works in this sculpture to emphasize the visual nature of the relationships of the parts and, thus, to offset any architectural, rather than sculptural, tendencies in the work.

The most powerful part of *The Window* is the space which it defines. That central vortex pulls the forms together around itself and imparts a circular, almost spiralling, rhythm to the piece. *Prairie* [29], in contrast, exists within the very center of a vortex, where there is complete

29. *Prairie*, 1967 (cf. illustration 43)

stillness and where ordinary, surrounding forces are suspended. The
four parallel steel tubes, which are painted a slightly lighter shade of matte
yellow ochre than the planes, seem to float without any need of support
and to touch the top edges of the diagonal planes without exerting any
pressure. Two of the tubes are, in fact, each supported only by a single
weld near one end and extend horizontally in opposing directions without
further interruption. The placement is virtuoso; the rhythm of the points
of contact, all far from the center, makes us look rapidly and repeatedly
from one end of the tubes to the other, attributing to the tubes, in the
process, forceful horizontal movement, throughout their lengths and beyond, which develops in the directions away from the points of contact
of each tube and moves toward their free ends, creating a momentum
which counteracts gravity. The four parallel channels of the corru-

gated steel plane, which itself seems to float, seem to register the weight
of four immaterial 'tubes' of space which run horizontally, perpendicular to the metal tubes, and which seem to press down into the corrugated
sheet, just as that sheet presses upward against them. The structure
of the sculpture is, however, perfectly straightforward. We can see clearly
that the corrugated sheet rests on the staggered diagonal planes, to
which, in turn, three of the tubes are welded. We can also see that the
tube closest to us is welded to an upright plane which is supported
and balanced by a horizontal strip that runs directly along the ground.
The whole configuration does not touch the rest of the sculpture but
is fully integrated within it visually through the parallelism of the tubes
and the sharing of the ground by the two parts of the work, the unify-
ing ground being articulated by the corresponding strips in the two sections. In reversal of the usual situation, our recognition of the technical
means of the sculpture makes *Prairie* even more astonishing than the illu-
sions which we had projected on to it made it seem, for *Prairie* exists,
on one level, in our space and on our ground and is subject to the
physical limitations to which we ourselves are subject. The sculpture
establishes itself as a perceived reality and makes illusion become
clearly a function of our own expectations. *Prairie* changes forever our
idea of what we can expect and gives us a new vision of the possible.

We have noted that during 1966 Caro's sculpture went through a
kind of refocusing. Concurrently, Caro became impatient with the fact
that a certain size had become so strongly associated with sculpture.
He thought it might be interesting to make some small sculptures which
would in no sense be studies or maquettes for larger works. These small
sculptures all share one characteristic that distinguishes them absolutely
from the large sculptures: namely, that they all reach beyond the limits
of the table surfaces on which they rest and extend below the level of that
surface, as the large sculptures, obviously, can never do on the ground.
The table pieces have a particular spirit of freedom and experimentation
that is often not possible in the large sculptures. The colors of the
painted table piece tend to be jazzy; sometimes the metal is polished,
glazed, or tempered rather than painted; and metals like brass and
bronze, not usually in Caro's vocabulary, have found their way into
some of the table pieces.

Table Piece XVIII [30], done in 1967, is, like most of the early table
pieces, made of polished steel. A cylinder, which lies on top of the
table and projects slightly beyond it, is connected by an S-form made of
two handles to a rectangle which seems to push against the side of
the table with a force as great as that with which the cylinder weighs

down against the top. The sculpture by no means simply rests on a 69
pedestal, but rather it questions the notion of being on anything and treats
the side of the table no differently than it treats the top, conventional
ideas about gravity and about which direction is up notwithstanding.

In *Table Piece XXII* [31], made of steel which is painted jewellescent
green, a stubby piece of curved pipe and a relatively long and thin
piece of tubing are both welded to a handle. We might consider this
sculpture in the light of a statement Caro made in 1961: 'I'm fed
up with objects on pedestals. I'd like to break down the graspability of
sculpture. Sculpture is terrifically tangible, but a painting, however
concrete, is partly in the realm of illusion.'[23] In many of the early table
pieces, Caro used handles – often scissors or tool handles – which state
the problem of graspability explicitly, almost teasingly. The handle in

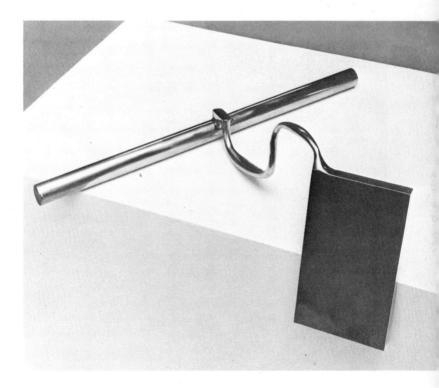

30. *Table Piece XVIII,* 1967

Table Piece XXII connects the curved pipe and the straight tubing in such a way that the forms, in that particular relationship to each other and to the surface of the table, seem to be immune to gravity, as evidenced especially by the position of the tube in relation to the table top. The fact of the sculpture's resting on the table is a prerequisite of that illusion and an essential condition in the logic of the piece. If we were to grasp the handle and lift the sculpture off the table, we would, in effect, destroy the sculpture, having taken away one of its parts – the table surface. (No specific table is ever associated with a sculpture; any flat raised surface will suffice.) By making the position of the sculpture on the table an integral part of the work, Caro has found a solution to the problem of graspability which radically removes his table pieces from the ordinary mode of objectness. In this respect, *Table Piece XXII* comes close

31. *Table Piece XXII*, 1967

to some of Jasper Johns's work, which is also concerned with the objectness of a work of art and the transformation of ordinary objects within a
work. The way in which the sculpture activates the table surface cuts
through the problem of the base with an eloquence unmatched even by
Brancusi's carved pedestals or David Smith's wheeled bases.

Table Piece XLII [32] is made of steel that has been polished and glazed
dark green. Within the scale of the piece, the forms are more solid
and blocky than Caro's forms usually are. Their solidity is, however,
offset by the extraordinary quality of the glaze, which makes the
color seem to permeate the forms, as if they were made of translucent
colored glass. There is a Bauhaus-like quality in the strict arrangement of the rectangular blocks, bar, and angle iron across the surface of
the table, softened only by two tangent, curving, but almost right-

32. *Table Piece XLII*, 1967

angle, lines. A thin line arches away from the confines of this rigid geo-
metry to an elongated rectangle which establishes a plane in space
that is independent of the table surface.

After David Smith's death in 1965, Caro acquired a sizable portion of
Smith's stockpile of steel forms. Among the forms was a number of
boiler tank tops, such as Smith used in his Tank Totem series. *Argentine*
[33], a large, grayish purple sculpture which Caro made in 1968, uses
two large pieces that were cut from a tank top, one piece placed upright
and the other propped up by a small, upright rectangle and leaning
toward the ground, like one of the planes in *Pompadour* [12]. That early
sculpture is quite frontal, and its expansion is primarily lateral. The two
sections of tank top in *Argentine*, however, create a strong central
focus, out of which the other forms develop eccentrically. A low,

33. *Argentine*, 1968

curving plane which emerges from behind the upright tank section echoes both the support of the other tank section and the sensuous, curving lines which seem to peel away from each other as they extend along the ground far from the center formed by the slow, swirling movement of the tank sections around the axis of their juncture. If we say that the mood of *Pompadour* is elegant, then we might say that the mood of *Argentine* is voluptuous.

Trefoil [34], which is painted the same matte yellow as the tubes in *Prairie* [29], reflects the concerns which Caro developed in his table pieces. *Trefoil* incorporates into its structure a large, square plane which is parallel to the ground and above, below, through, and around which the other forms in the sculpture move. One upright straight bar seems to pass through the plane as if it were immaterial, while a high arc seems

34. *Trefoil*, 1968

to rebound off the plane in a long, low arc. An arc which originates under
the plane ricochets off the ground into the space beside the plane. The
plane's means of support are sufficiently dispersed so that it seems to float
in space, and the way in which forms seem to penetrate through the
plane, and to bounce off it, give it an ambiguous solidity. One straight
bar seems to be deflected into a curve as it passes through the plane,
as if the space beneath the plane were somehow denser than the space
above it. At two of the sculpture's points of contact with the ground
there are rebounds of disproportionate magnitude. The ground becomes
an unpredictable, active element in the sculpture, and we begin to
wonder whether the ground is as equivocal and enigmatic as the sup-
posedly solid plane above it. Might the arc which does not rebound
off the ground continue on through the ground?

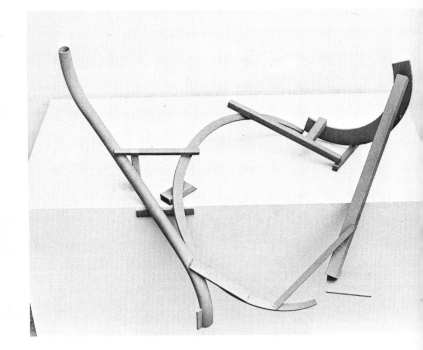

35. *Table Piece LXIV*, 1968

Table Piece LXIV [35] is an intricate table sculpture, which is painted
the same color as *Trefoil*. The sculpture is particularly unusual in that Caro
did not remove the tack bars, which ordinarily only hold the parts
together during the process of construction and welding, but which now
become an integral part of the work. Straight and curving lines play off
against each other in a configuration which rests on the table surface,
balances on the table edge, and spills out into the space beyond and below
the table. This sculpture is reminiscent of David Smith's small silver
sculpture *Timeless Clock* of 1957, a metal 'drawing' which resembles
Caro's piece except for the fact that Smith's piece stands upright in
space and is mounted on a small base.

After Summer [36A, B] is a great, huge, chthonic, apocalyptic sculpture,
painted a matte greenish grey, in which four pairs of quadrants, cut

36A. *After Summer*, in construction, 1968   36B *(overleaf)*. *After Summer*, 1968

from the boiler tops, billow outward along a groundwork of two long
bars and a series of crosspieces. In its ground plan and its combination
of rigid, skeletal structure with sensuous form, *After Summer* resembles
a medieval nave, with its directed and extended space and its rhythm of
pillars and arches. (While at the Royal Academy Schools, Caro once
spent a month studying the cathedral at Chartres.[24]) In elevation, however, *After Summer* differs greatly from a cathedral. Its expansion is
lateral, rather than vertical, and its lowest elevation is along the central
longitudinal axis. (The sculpture is only five feet high, but twenty-four
feet long and almost twenty feet wide.) The first pair of quadrants draws
us into the piece, while the second pair blocks our visual progress
momentarily. These first two pairs together partly enclose a kind of ante-
chamber, a solemn and anticipatory space through which our gaze

must pass before reaching the revelatory space dominated by the third pair of quadrants, which do not touch each other a few inches above the ground, as the other quadrants do, but which rest directly on the ground, separated from each other by an open space. A portion of these quadrants is cut away, so that they seem more to arch than to swell outward to the smaller fragments of tank tops to which they are connected, extending laterally like a transept that offers release from the channelled longitudinal progression, realizing the expansive tension of the quadrants against the linear framework, and breaking away from the rigid symmetry of the rest of the forms. The fourth pair of quadrants echoes the form and direction of the first pair and, by association, returns us, changed, having experienced the climax of the sculpture, to those first quadrants in a movement that is ambiguously cyclical and open-ended.

After Summer was the last sculpture that was included in the major
retrospective of Caro's work that was organized by the Arts Council of
Great Britain and shown in the Hayward Gallery in London from
January to March 1969. After that chance to see the major accomplish-
ments of almost a decade's work brought together and to reconsider
where he had come from and where he had travelled, Caro proceeded on
his way, changed, perhaps, by the review of his work, but also essentially the same.

Table Piece LXXV [37], one of the first table sculptures done after the show,
embodies the kind of change and motion around a center that we have
noted before in Caro's work. A slightly twisting, broad steel form, rounded
at one end and more or less squared at the other, is half on and half
off the surface of the table. Two curving forms move around the central

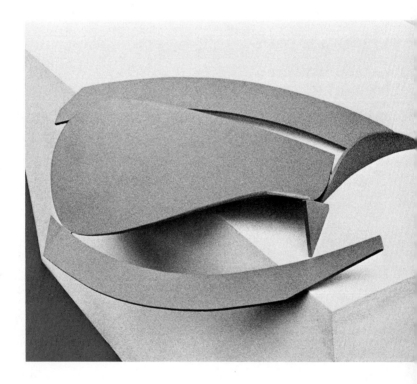

37. *Table Piece LXXV*, 1969

form like the arms of a barred spiral galaxy, one connected directly to
the rounded end of the central form and curving through space onto the
table, the other connected through a small, curved form, pointed at
both ends, to the squared end of the central form and curving along the
table surface until it just barely projects over the edge. A small
triangle connected to the squared end of the central form almost touches
the table; and the second arm almost touches the round end of the central form as it goes off the table. The dualities of the sculpture – round and
square, on the table and off the table, touching and not touching – are
concentrated in the single central form, around which other forms revolve.

Table Piece LXXXVIII [38] is an extraordinarily complex and turbulent
sculpture, in which the forms seem to be frozen in a moment of
cataclysm. The subtitle of the piece, *Deluge*, refers, as John Russell has

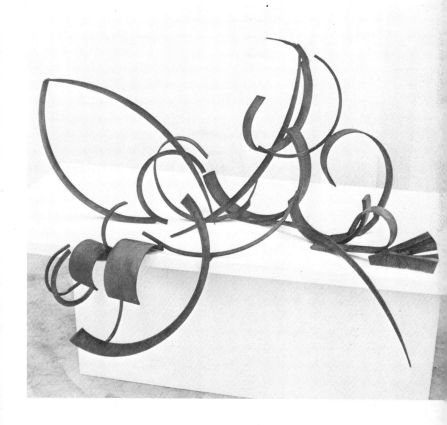

38. *Table Piece LXXXVIII*, 1969

suggested,[25] to the Leonardo drawings of deluges that were exhibited
at the Queen's Gallery in London in 1969. Kenneth Clark has said
of those drawings: 'They express, with a freedom which is almost dis-
turbing, [Leonardo's] passion for twisting movement, and for sequences
of form fuller and more complex than anything in European art . . . Only
in Oriental art do we find a similar mastery of the convention, by
which forces and directions are reduced to visible linear curves.'[26] The
linear curves of *Deluge* swirl and leap in every direction, often curving
back on themselves or seeming to move simultaneously both upward and
downward or both inward and outward, so that the forces by which
they seem to be possessed always operate within an uncanny equilibrium.
The elements of the sculpture are so numerous and their interrelationships so complex that no single form can ever become separate; in de-
scribing the sculpture, we can only speak of the whole, not of individual
forms. The wildly divergent forces of the sculpture are subsumed into a
single phenomenon, in the ironic unity of which problems of balance
and composition disappear. It is precisely because of its chaos that the
sculpture coheres so completely. In the deluge, the instant of chaos,
the work and ourselves are made whole.

Notes

1. Herbert Read, *A Concise History of Modern Sculpture*, London, 1966, p. 178. First published in the *Listener*, 18 August 1937.
2. For much of the biographical information given in this essay I am in-debted to John Russell, 'Portrait: Anthony Caro', *Art in America*, September–October 1966, pp. 80–87, and Sheila Caro, biographical note, catalogue of Caro's show at the Whitechapel Gallery, London, 1963.
3. Anthony Caro, 'Henry Moore, an appreciation', London, *Observer*, 27 November 1960.
4. ibid.
5. Illustrated in John Russell, op. cit.
6. See Michael Fried's introduction to the catalogue of Caro's retrospective at the Hayward Gallery, London, 1969.
7. Heinrich Wölfflin, *Classic Art*, London, 1959, p. 194.
8. Walter J. Ong, SSJ, *The Presence of the World*, New Haven, 1967, pp. 117–18.
9. Michael Fried, op. cit., p. 6.
10. ibid., pp. 6–7.
11. Herbert Read, *A Concise History of Modern Sculpture*, New York, 1964, p. 88.
12. Reyner Banham, 'The World of the Brutalists, Opinion and Intention in British Architecture, 1951–1960', *Texas Quarterly*, Autumn, 1961, p. 132.
13. Michael Fried has said that 'the visual initiative which [Caro's] pieces call for is more like listening to than like looking at'.
14. Wallace Stevens, *Poems*, ed. S. F. Morse, New York, 1959.
15. Clement Greenberg, *Art and Culture*, Boston, 1965, p. 144.
16. Michael Fried, op. cit., p. 7.
17. Andrew Forge, Interview with Anthony Caro, *Studio International*, January 1966, p. 8.
18. John Russell, 'The Triumph of Anthony Caro', *The Sunday Times*, London, 26 January, 1969.
19. Hans Hofmann, in *The Search for the Real and Other Essays*, ed. by Sarah T. Weeks and Bartlett H. Hayes, Jr, Addison Gallery of American Art, Andover, Massachusetts, 1948.
20. Lawrence Alloway, Interview with Anthony Caro, *Gazette*, London, no. 1, 1961.
21. Donald Judd, 'Specific Objects', *Arts Yearbook*, no. 8, 1965, p. 78.
22. Lawrence Alloway, op. cit.
23 ibid.

24. John Russell, 'Portrait: Anthony Caro', op. cit. 82.
25. John Russell, 'Closing the Gaps', *Art News*, May 1970. (See pp. 111–13 below.)
26. Kenneth Clark, *Leonardo da Vinci*, Harmondsworth, 1959, p. 151.

Selected Bibliography

I have included in this bibliography only items which I consider to be particularly interesting and worthwhile. For a more comprehensive bibliography, the reader is referred to the catalogue of Caro's retrospective at the Hayward Gallery, London, 1969. [R.W.]

Alloway, Lawrence, 'Caro and gravity'. Foreword to exhibition catalogue, Galleria del Naviglio, Milan, 1956.

Alloway, Lawrence, Interview with Anthony Caro, *Gazette*, no. 1, London, 1961.

Annesley, David, Louw, Roelof, Scott, Tim, and Tucker, William, 'Anthony Caro's work: a symposium by four sculptors', *Studio International*, vol. 177, no. 907, January 1969, pp. 14–20.

Baro, Gene, 'A look at reminiscence: Paolozzi and Caro', *Arts Magazine*, vol. 38, no. 2, November 1963, pp. 44–7.

Baro, Gene, 'Britain's new sculpture', *Art International*, vol. 9, no. 5, June 1965, pp. 26–31.

Baro, Gene, 'British sculpture: the developing scene', *Studio International*, vol. 172, no. 882, October 1966, pp. 171–81.

Benedikt, Michael, 'New York Letter', *Art International*, vol. 11, no. 1, January 1967, p. 56.

Cone, Jane Harrison, 'Caro in London', *Artforum*, vol. 7, no. 8, April 1969, pp. 62–6.

Forge, Andrew, Interview with Anthony Caro, *Studio International*, vol. 171, no. 873, January 1966, pp. 6–9.

Fried, Michael, 'Anthony Caro', *Art International*, vol. 7, no. 7, 25 September 1963, pp. 68–71. [Reprint of Whitechapel catalogue introduction].

Fried, Michael, 'New Work by Anthony Caro', *Artforum*, vol. 5, no. 6, February 1967, pp. 46–7.

Fried, Michael, 'Art and Objecthood', *Artforum*, vol. 5, no. 10, Summer 1967, pp. 12–23.

Fried, Michael, 'Two Sculptures by Anthony Caro', *Artforum*, vol. 6, no. 6, February 1968, pp. 24–5. (See pp. 95–101 below.)

Fried, Michael, Introduction to exhibition catalogue, Hayward Gallery, London, 1969.

Greenberg, Clement, 'Anthony Caro', *Contemporary Sculpture*, Arts Yearbook 8, 1965, pp. 106–9. (See pp. 87–93 below.)

Greenberg, Clement, 'David Smith', *Art in America*, vol. 54, no. 1, January–February 1966, pp. 27–32.

Greenberg, Clement, 'Recentness of Sculpture', Introduction to exhibition catalogue, *American Sculpture of the Sixties*, Los Angeles County Museum of Art, 1967. [Reprinted in *Art International*, vol. 11, no. 4, 20 April 1967 pp. 19–21.]

Harrison, Charles, 'Some recent sculpture in Britain', *Studio International*, vol. 177, no. 907, January 1969, pp. 26–33.

Harrison, Charles, 'Anthony Caro', Introduction to exhibition catalogue, British Pavilion, X Bienal de São Paulo, 1969.

Kramer, Hilton, 'Anthony Caro: a gifted sculptor within a tradition', *New York Times*, 9 November 1968.

Kramer, Hilton, 'A Promise of Greatness', *New York Times*, 17 May 1970.

Krauss, Rosalind, 'On Anthony Caro's latest work', *Art International*, vol. 11, no. 1, January 1967, pp. 26–9.

Reichardt, Jasia, 'Caro and environmental sculpture', *Architectural Design*, vol. 23, no. 10, October 1963, p. 454.

Reichardt, Jasia, 'Colour in sculpture', *Quadrum*, no. 18, 1965, pp. 71–8.

Robertson, Bryan, Preface to exhibition catalogue, Whitechapel Gallery, 1963.

Robertson, Bryan, Preface to exhibition catalogue, 'The New Generation', Whitechapel Gallery, 1965.

Russell, John, 'Portrait: Anthony Caro', *Art in America*, vol. 54, no. 5, September–October 1966, pp. 80–87.

Russell, John, 'Triumph of Anthony Caro', *Sunday Times*, London, 26 January 1969.

Russell, John, 'Closing the Gaps', *Art News*, vol. 69, no. 3, May 1970, pp. 37–9. (See pp. 111–13 below.)

Sylvester, David, 'Aspects of Contemporary British Art', *Texas Quarterly*, vol. 4, no. 3, Autumn 1961, pp. 118–28.

Thompson, David, 'Venice Biennale: the British five', *Studio International*, vol. 171, no. 878, June 1966, 233–43.

Clement Greenberg

Michael Fried

John Russell

Phyllis Tuchman

Clement Greenberg: Anthony Caro

'Breakthrough' is a much-abused word in contemporary art writing, but I don't hesitate to apply it to the sculpture in steel that Anthony Caro, of London, has been doing since 1960. During the fifties, abstract sculpture seemed to go pretty much where David Smith took it. None of the promises made by other sculptors during that time was really fulfilled; some of them produced good things, but the good things remained isolated, did not add up. Caro is the only sculptor who has definitely emerged from this situation and, in emerging from it,

39. *Sculpture Two*, 1962 (cf. illustration 8)

begun to change it. He is the only new sculptor whose sustained quality can bear comparison with Smith's. With him it has become possible at long last to talk of a generation in sculpture that really comes after Smith's.

Caro is also the first sculptor to digest Smith's ideas instead of merely borrowing from them. Precisely by deriving from Smith he has been the better able to establish his own individuality. Unquestionably, he was led to the use of ready-made materials by Smith's example, which may also have shown him how it was possible to achieve 'free' effects with geometrical elements. But Caro's sculptures invade space in a quite different way – a way that is as different almost from Smith's as it is from Gonzalez' – and they are more integrally abstract. Caro is far less interested in contours or profiles than in vectors, lines of force and direction. Rarely does a single shape in Caro's sculpture give satisfaction in itself; the weight of his art lies preponderantly in what Michael Fried calls its 'syntax', that is, in the relations of its discrete parts. In his catalogue text for the first show of Caro's post-1959 work at the Whitechapel Gallery in London in September and October of 1963 (the text is reprinted in *Art International*, vol. 7, no. 7, 25 September 1963), Mr Fried writes: 'Everything in Caro's art that is worth looking at – except the color – is in its syntax.' This emphasis on syntax is also an emphasis on abstractness, on radical unlikeness to nature.

No other sculptor has gone as far from the structural logic of ordinary ponderable things. Certainly not Calder, whose mobiles so obviously evoke plant forms with their spinal and nodal symmetries. Symmetry enters Caro's art too, but only at the last moment as it were, surreptitiously and indirectly. Planar and linear shapes of steel (there are no solidly enclosed volumes in Caro's vocabulary) gather together in what the surprised eye takes at first for mere agglomerations. Seldom is there an enclosing silhouette or internal pattern with readily apparent axes and centers of interest; these, when they emerge, do so tangentially and ex-centrically. That the ground plan will at times echo as well as interlock with the superstructure or elevation (as in the superb *Sculpture Two* of 1962 [39]) only renders the unity of a piece that much harder to grasp at first. Yet just those factors that make for confusion at first make most for unity in the end.

Despite all that it owes to pictorial art, and despite its radical rejection of monolithic structure, Caro's work is less pictorial than Smith's. His pieces ask to be looked at from many different, and dramatically different, points of view; and in some cases the spectator has to look *down* as

well as straight ahead. Caro's 'roundness' is the more paradoxical because
there is so little in his vocabulary of forms that leads the eye into depth.
Almost all surfaces and edges are rectilinear, and almost all their changes
of direction are strictly rectangular. Far from being anything like cal-
ligraphic, Caro's drawing is not even cursive (it shies away from curved
forms the way British engineering design tends to, or used to tend to).
But the relationships of the rectangular details in Caro's sculpture, while
necessarily angular, are themselves only sparingly *rect*angular: it is as
if the rectangular were set up in one aspect only to be the more tellingly
countered in another. By the tilting, tipping and odd-angle cantilever-
ing of his rectangular shapes Caro achieves a kind of sprawling cursiveness
that is all his own, and which makes everything that would otherwise
look separate and frontal move and fuse.

The play of light against heavy is interwoven, fugally, with the play of
open against closed, and of irregular against regular. Or at least this
is so in most of the steel sculpture that Caro did at home in England. Five
of the seven pieces he made in America during 1963–4 (while
teaching at Bennington College) show a marked change of manner in
which lightness and regularity override nearly everything else. Relationships become almost altogether rectangular and boxlike, and there
is a plain, emphasized symmetry. This forthright symmetry has a
startling effect insofar as it suggests a syntactic massiveness, so to speak,
that takes over the work of the literal massiveness of heavy steel in
Caro's English-made sculpture. Caro's American pieces are for the most
part smaller and made of much lighter and thinner steel, but the
foursquare squatness that is imposed on them by their rectangular symmetry makes them look less fragile than one would expect. The spec-
tacular inner and outer play of Caro's English-made sculpture is missing,
but the effect is almost as new intrinsically.

Nothing of the preceding applies to Caro's two last American-made
works *Titan* [40] and *Bennington* [41], which he finished before his return
to London in June of 1964. These are perhaps more purely, more
limpidly, masterpieces than anything he has done before. In them that
search for a low center of gravity which is one of the most constant
features of his originality finds a perfect fulfillment. Ground-flung, wide-
open enclosures (in 'L' and 'T' form respectively) that are relieved by
two or three vertical elements no more than four feet high, the two pieces
strike the heroic, grand-manner note even more resonantly than the
best of Caro's large English sculptures do. I say more resonantly, because
less expectedly, less in terms of the historic connotations of the grand

manner. (Though Caro's roots in English art tradition – roots that go back
literally to Perpendicular Gothic – become more evident the longer
one looks. A grand, sublime manner has been a peculiarly English aspir-
ation since the eighteenth century. Henry Moore and Francis Bacon
are possessed by it in their separate ways just as much as Haydon, John
Martin and even Turner were in theirs. Without maintaining necessarily that he is a better artist than Turner, I would venture to say that
Caro comes closer to a genuine grand manner – genuine because
original and unsynthetic – than any English artist before him.)

Michael Fried speaks aptly of Caro's 'achieved weightlessness'. It is a
kind of weightlessness that belongs, distinctively, to the new tradition of non-monolithic sculpture which has sprung from the Cubist collage. Part of Caro's originality of style consists in denying weight by

40. *Titan*, 1964 (cf. illustration 15)

lowering as well as by raising the things in his sculpture that signify it.
The pre-war Giacometti had a glimpse of this possibility, but only a
glimpse, even though he made several masterpieces from it. Caro works
the possibility out. By opening and extending a ground-hugging sculpture laterally, and inflecting it vertically in a way that accents the lateral
movement, the plane of the ground is made to seem to move too; it
ceases being the base or foil against which everything else moves, and
takes its own part in the challenge to the force of gravity.

Applied color is another of the means to weightlessness in Caro's art,
as Michael Fried, again, points out. It acts – especially in the high-
keyed off-shades that Caro favors – to deprive metal surfaces of their
tactile connotations and render them more 'optical'. I grant the
essential importance to Caro's art of color in this role, but this is not

to say that I, for one, find his color satisfactory. I know of no piece
of his, not even an unsuccessful one, that does not transcend its color,
or whose *specific* color or combination of colors does not detract
from the quality of the whole (especially when there is more than one
color). In every case I have the impression that the color is aesthe-
tically (as well as literally) provisional – that it can be changed at will
without decisively affecting quality. Here, as almost everywhere else
in post-Gothic Western sculpture, color remains truly the 'secondary' pro-
perty that philosophers used to think color in general was . . .

It ought to be unnecessary to say that Caro's originality is more than
a question of stylistic or formal ingenuity. Were it that, it would
amount to no more than novelty, and taste would not, in the event,
find itself so challenged by it. Caro's art is original because it

41. *Bennington*, 1964 (cf. illustration 16)

changes and expands taste in order to make room for itself. And it
is able to do this only because it is the product of a necessity;
only because it is compelled by a vision that is unable to make itself
known except by changing art.   [1965]

Michael Fried: Two Sculptures by Anthony Caro

Deep Body Blue [42], the smaller of the two pieces in Anthony Caro's
recent show at the Kasmin Gallery, is open as wide-spread arms and then
as a door is open. The two contrasting elements that run along the
ground, a length of tubing and a flat sheet standing on its long edge,
gather the beholder into a far more compelling embrace than could
be achieved by literally embracing him – the way, for example, one is
embraced by Bernini's colonnades in front of St Peter's – while the
two uprights are experienced as a kind of abstract door on the other side
of which two similarly contrasting elements converge, touch, and go

42. *Deep Body Blue*, 1967

their ways. Like several recent sculptures by Caro, *Deep Body Blue* explores
possibilities for sculpture in various concepts and experiences which
one would think belonged today only to architecture: *e.g.*, those of being
led up to something, of entering it, perhaps by going through something else, of being inside something, of looking out from within . . . Not
that Caro's work is architectural in look or essence. But it shares with
architecture preoccupation with the fact, or with the implications of the
fact, that men have bodies and live in a physical world. This preoccupation finds a natural, and inescapably literal, home in architecture.
The same preoccupation no longer finds a *natural* home in painting
and sculpture; it is the nearly impossible task of artists like Caro to put
it there; and this can only be done by rendering it *anti*-literal or (what
I mean by) *abstract*. The heart of Caro's genius is that he is able to make
radically abstract sculpture out of concepts and experiences which
seem – which but for his making are and would remain – inescapably
literal and therefore irremediably theatrical; and by so doing he re-
deems the time if anyone does. Not only is the radical abstractness of
Caro's art not a denial of our bodies and the world. It is the only
way in which they can be saved for high art in our time, in which they
can be made present to us other than as theater.

   In the course of his enterprise Caro makes discoveries as sudden and
as exhilarating as any in modern philosophy. For example, it is essential to our experiencing the two uprights in *Deep Body Blue* as a kind
of door that they stand in the same plane. It doesn't matter that they
are no more than four feet high, that they lack any sort of lintel, that we
are not tempted or even able to pass between them: the fact that they
stand several feet apart in the same plane is enough to make us experience them as an abstract door (and a wide one at that). By the same
token, if they are moved even very slightly out of alignment their 'door-
ness' disintegrates and the sculpture as a whole begins to fall apart,
to become arbitrary and therefore meaningless as art. This aspect of Caro's
achievement may be described in several ways. One can say that he
discovered what constitutes an *abstract* door; or that he discovered the
essence of a door; or that he discovered the *conventions* – corresponding to deep needs – which make something a door. Caro did not consciously set out to discover anything of the kind. On the contrary,
it is because *Deep Body Blue* began in a preoccupation with particular
modes of being in the world that its very success as sculpture came
to depend on the making of the above discovery in, or by, the piece itself. It is as though with Caro sculpture itself has become commit-

ted to a new kind of cognitive enterprise: not because its generating impulse has become philosophical, but because the newly explicit need to defeat theater in all its manifestations has meant that the ambition to make sculpture out of a primordial involvement with modes of being in the world can now be realized *only* if anti-literal – that is, radically abstract – terms for that involvement can be found. (At the risk of seeming to overload a point, I will add that the cognitive enterprise in question is related, in different ways, both to European phenomenology and to the later philosophy of Wittgenstein. It isn't only modernist *art* that has found it necessary to defeat theater.)

The larger sculpture, *Prairie* [43], consists of four long poles of aluminum tubing suspended parallel to one another about eleven inches above a sheet of corrugated metal – more exactly, a flat sheet with four channel-like depressions in it – which runs north-south to the poles' east-west and is itself suspended about twenty-one inches above the ground. If we approach *Prairie* from either end of that sheet, the physical means by which these suspensions are accomplished are not apparent; but as we move around the sculpture it becomes clear that the sheet is held up by two sharply-bent pieces of metal plate, one on each side, which spring out and down from the underside of the sheet until they touch the ground, whereupon they angle upward and outward until they reach the height of the poles, which they support also. Two of the poles are supported at only one point, about twenty inches from the end; a third is supported about twenty inches from both ends, that is, by both of the bent, upward-springing metal plates; while a fourth is not supported by these at all but is held up by a large, upright rectangle of metal which stands somewhat apart from the rest of the sculpture and in fact is not physically connected to it in any way. But grasping exactly how *Prairie* works as a feat of engineering does not in the least undermine or even compete with one's initial impression that the metal poles and corrugated sheet are suspended, as if in the absence of gravity, at different levels above the ground. Indeed, the ground itself is seen, not as that upon which everything else stands and from which everything else rises, but rather as the last, or *lowest*, of the three levels which, as abstract conception, *Prairie* comprises. (In this sense *Prairie* defines the ground, not as that which ultimately supports everything else, but as that which does not itself require support. It makes this fact about the ground both phenomenologically surprising and sculpturally significant.)

The result is an extraordinary marriage of illusion and structural obviousness. Once we have walked even partly around *Prairie* there is nothing we do not know about how it supports itself, and yet that knowledge is somehow put in abeyance by our actual experience of the piece as sculpture. It is as though in *Prairie*, as often in Caro's work, illusion is not achieved at the expense of physicality so much as it exists simultaneously with it in such a way that, in the grip of the piece, we do not see past the first to the second. This is mostly due to the nature of the relationships among the various elements that compose *Prairie*, relationships which make a different kind of sense to the mind and to the eye. For example, that three of the long metal poles are held up at only one end is *understood* to mean that the full weight of each pole is borne by a single support far from its center; but the poles are *seen* as being in a state of balance as they are, as if they weighed nothing and could be placed anywhere without support. This impression is

43. *Prairie*, 1967 (cf. illustration 29)

reinforced by the fact that the two poles supported at one end by a bent,
upward-springing metal plate are held up by different plates and at
opposite ends. Similarly, the one pole supported at both ends is held up
by the far corner of the nearer plate and by the near corner of the
farther one; and this deliberate staggering, while perfectly understood
by the mind, disconcerts the eye enough to make it see that pole
as if it were not truly supported at all. That all four poles are parallel
to and equidistant from one another, and that three of them are
the same length, are other factors which obstruct the eye from giving
weight to the specific means by which each is supported. (It should
also be said that the fact that the four poles are an almost imperceptibly
lighter shade of sandy yellow than the rest of the sculpture gives them
an added suggestion of lift.) In these and other ways Caro on the one hand

has frankly avowed the physicality of his sculpture and on the other has rendered that physicality unperspicuous to a degree that even after repeated viewings is barely credible. This is not in itself a new development in his work; it has been a steady feature of his art since his conversion to radical abstraction around 1959. But it reaches in *Prairie* an extreme that may also be a kind of culmination. More explicitly than any previous sculpture, *Prairie* compels us to believe what we see rather than what we know, to accept the witness of the senses against the construction of the mind.

Finally, Caro has never before sought openness in abstract *extension* as here. For the first time the openness which Caro achieves is above all a *lateral* openness – with the result that we are made to feel that lateralness as such is open in a way that verticality or obliqueness or head-on recession are not. This is a point of deep affinity between *Prairie* and the superb paintings in Kenneth Noland's last show at the Emmerich Gallery, in which the lateral extension of the canvas and its colors accomplished, among other things, an apparent liberation from the constrictions of the picture-shape. In both *Prairie* and Noland's paintings the decisive experience is one of instantaneous extension, roughly from somewhere in the middle of the poles or canvas out towards both ends. In each the exact dimensions of what is extended laterally is of crucial importance: if either the poles or the canvas were too long or short, the result would be a flaccid or blocky objecthood. (Objecthood of one kind or another is in effect the aim of literalist work, which does not begin or end so much as it merely stops, and in which an indefinite – by implication, infinite – progression takes place as if in time.) Caro seems to have faced the further risk that *Prairie* might be too open, at any rate that the eye might be compelled away from the piece itself into the space around it, in which case it would strike one less as open than as flimsy or insufficient. That this does not occur is due to Caro's use of the solid rectangle of metal which supports the fourth pole: placed largely beyond the previous limits of the sculpture, it actually extends the sculpture at the same time as it helps contain its energies by giving the eye something flat, vertical and opaque to come up against. The lack of physical connection between the rectangle-and-pole ensemble and the rest of the piece has been made as unperspicuous as the precise character of the connections among the other elements – another reason why *Prairie* is by far the most successful sculpture in two or more parts that I have ever seen.

I believe that *Prairie* is a masterpiece, one of the great works of modern art, a touchstone for future sculpture, and that *Deep Body Blue*, while less ambitious, is nevertheless beyond the reach of any other sculptor alive. In the radicalness of their abstraction both have more in common with certain poetry and music, and certain recent painting, than with the work of any previous sculptor. And yet this very radicalness enables them to achieve a body and a world of meaning and expression that belong essentially to sculpture.   [1968]

Michael Fried: Caro's Abstractness

Orangerie [44], one of the most ravishing sculptures Caro has ever made, is also one of the most nearly pictorial. Unlike most of his pieces it appears to comprise a number of discrete and rather highly characterized *shapes*, whose mutual juxtaposition, while not actually establishing a single plane or a succession of planes, seems nevertheless to imply the kind of planarity we associate with painting. (It is right that Matisse has been mentioned in connection with Caro's recent work. The affinity between *Orangerie* and the art of Morris Louis, for example the so-called

44. *Orangerie*, 1969

Aleph paintings, might also be noted.) And yet how un-pictorial *Orangerie* finally is. The chief rounded shapes delineate themselves above all by twisting in space. Its seeming planarity is in the end decisively subverted by the angling and arcing – the rapid, curved-versus-straight cursiveness in depth – both of individual elements and of the 'ground plan' as a whole. Most important *Orangerie* must be seen in relation to Caro's table-sculptures, which he has been making more or less steadily since the summer of 1966, and as a step beyond the superb *Trefoil* (1968) [34], in which he first physically included the plane of the table in a sculpture that stands on the ground.

Briefly, the ambition behind the table-sculptures was to make small works that could not be seen merely as reduced versions of larger ones – sculptures whose smallness was to be secured abstractly, made part of their essence, instead of remaining simply a literal, quantitative fact about them. That ambition led Caro, first, to incorporate handles of various kinds in most of his early table-sculptures, in an attempt to key the scale of each piece to that of graspable and manipulable objects (partial precedents for this include Picasso's *Glass of Absinthe* and a few sculptures by Giacometti); and second, to run or set at least one element in every piece *below* the level of the table-top on which the sculpture was to be placed, thereby precluding its transposition, in fact or in imagination, to the ground. It at once turned out that by tabling, or precluding grounding, the sculptures in this way Caro was able to establish their smallness in terms that proved virtually independent of actual size. That is, the distinction between tabling and grounding, because determined (or acknowledged) by the sculptures themselves instead of merely imposed upon them by their eventual placement, made itself felt as equivalent to what may be thought of as a qualitative rather than quantitative difference in scale. (Not only has the abstract smallness of Caro's table-sculptures proved compatible with surprising largeness of actual size; it soon became apparent that a certain *minimum* size was required for their tabling to be experienced in these terms.) In these and other respects Caro's table-sculptures mark the emergence of a sense of scale for which there is no precedent in earlier sculpture and no clear parallel in our experience of the world. The incorporation in *Trefoil* of a table, or table-*top*, may be seen as merging largeness and smallness as both had come to be defined in and by Caro's art. While in *Orangerie* Caro has extended and refined the implications of such a merging of abstract scales by raising the already thin and narrow tabular plane almost to eye level, and by angling a second plane into

it from the front, which together largely attenuate its ostensive normativeness. The result is altogether more delicate and less obviously
table-like (more shelf-like?) than in *Trefoil*. But once again it is to the
tabular plane even more than to the ground that the other elements chiefly relate.

The exploitation of different levels, basic to Caro's abstract sculptures
from the first, is also crucial to the other indisputably major work –
Deep North [45]. In that sculpture a rectangular piece of heavy grid is
suspended parallel to the ground at a height of about eight feet in
a way that allows, but does not compel, the beholder to position himself beneath it. This may appear to break with what has been one
of the fundamental norms of Caro's art: the refusal to allow the beholder
to enter a given work, to step or stand inside it. That refusal has been

45. *Deep North*, 1969–70

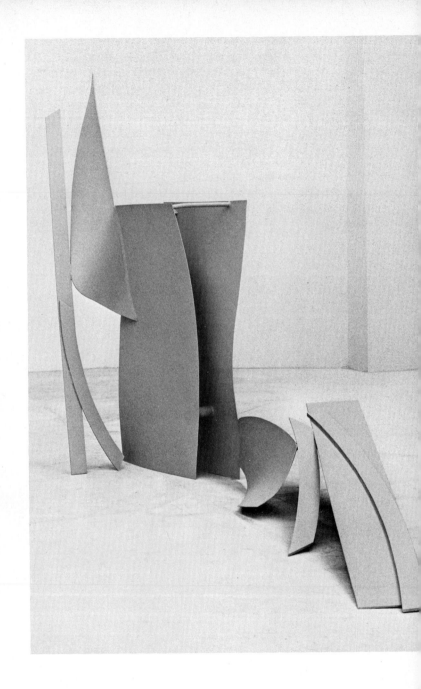

46. *Sun Runner*, 1969

striking both because of the general openness of Caro's sculptures, and more particularly because of the manifest preoccupation of certain pieces (I do not say of Caro himself) with experiences such as entering, going through, being enclosed, looking out from within, etc., which one might have thought would virtually have entailed a kind of environmentalism. Moreover, the obduracy of Caro's sculptures on this score has been only one aspect, though an important one, of their anti-literal, anti-situational character; and *that* has been an index at once of their radical abstractness and of their deep antagonism to the theatrical in all its current forms and manifestations. So that by allowing us actually to stand beneath a portion of itself, *Deep North* may appear to call into question, perhaps even to renounce, what has been until now the essence of Caro's art.

But the facts of experience do not bear this out. Even when we place ourselves directly beneath the massive grid we do not feel that we have entered or that we are inside the sculpture. Partly this has to do with the nature of something *overhead*: if we were compelled to step over or across some sort of boundary, however low or slight, the sensation of entering would, I think, become inescapable – though once again the exact basis of this in our experience of the world remains obscure. Partly too it is a function of the way in which every element in the piece seems to twist, turn, face, point or open *away* from every other. And partly it stems from the fact that *Deep North*'s vital center, from which the sculpture as a whole is felt to originate, is located far from the grid and its supports, *i.e.*, at the ground-level juncture of the three other principal elements, and that our view from beneath the grid both of that juncture and of the relations between those elements (in particular the inspired rhymes among them), if not actually privileged, is at any rate profoundly satisfying. We are of course aware of not seeing *all* of the sculpture – specifically, of not seeing the grid itself – when standing beneath the latter. But this is experienced as nothing more than a special instance of the limitations inherent in *any* point of view. In this respect *Deep North* belongs with *After Summer* (1968) [36A, B], which partly because of its great size conspicuously resists being seen in its entirety from any single position. None of this is to deny that an apprehension of the grid as overhead, as a kind of roof or ceiling under which we can stand, dominates our experience of the sculpture as a whole. What must be insisted upon is that this is true whether or not we choose to station ourselves beneath the grid: it is a function, not of any literal or architectural relationship between structure and beholder, but of the internal relations (or syntax) of the sculpture alone,

47 (overleaf). Sun Feast, 1969–70

relations which however are deeply grounded in the nature and potentialities of the human body.

The large yellow *Sun Feast* [47] may be more complex and at bottom more difficult of access than either *Orangerie* or *Deep North*. There are, in any case, at least three types of order at work in it. First, that of Caro's table-sculptures and their subsumption in pieces like *Trefoil* and *Orangerie*. The long horizontal plank that runs almost the full length of the sculpture serves as the 'table' on top of which various elements are placed and off of which these and other elements depend or spring or otherwise make their way. Second, the play of elements along and against a dominant axis or track, also identified with the long horizontal plank. This organizing principle appeared in Caro's work as early as the great *Midday* [6], a piece that has much in common with *Sun Feast*.

And third, a kind of sensuous, disheveled, almost certainly feminine though not quite figural sprawl, as if the sculpture were displaying itself for its own delectation. The combination of intellectual rigor and intense sensuality again recalls Matisse. But it is also wholly characteristic of Caro's Blakean imagination. If *Sun Feast* has a fault, and it may not, it is perhaps too much reliance on the curvilinear, which makes for an effect of great elegance and disguises the sculpture's underlying difficulty – the difficulty, for example, of the coexistence of several modes of order, no one of which is entirely satisfying, or of the contrast between the thickness of most of the piece and the unnerving thinness of the twisting, ploughshare-like elements disposed along the horizontal plank.

Wending Back [48] is the smallest and in obvious respects the least ambitious of the sculptures discussed here. But it could not be better and

ought to be recognized for what it is, a small masterpiece. No less inert, more energized, in abstract terms more kinetic sculpture can be imagined. It is as though Caro constructed *Wending Back* directly out of brief but articulate segments of trajectories, vectors, torques. Everything sweeps, scoops, slices and is sliced. Even the triangular shape of the largest element seems the result of three shearing arcs whose full dimensions we can only guess. And in general *Wending Back* implies magnitudes of energy and extension that far exceed its physical limits. Perhaps because of this, the stabilizing, *grounding* normativeness of the narrow rectangular element that stands on edge is vital to its success. The dark grey color, too, resists the dematerialization implicit in *Wending Back*'s kinetic syntax, and by so doing further collects the sculpture as a whole while making the abstract nature of its energies all the more self-evident.

[1970]

48. *Wending Back*, 1969

John Russell: Closing the Gaps

Big art comes about when the gap is closed, conclusively, between what can be said already and what needs to be said today. Anthony Caro did this consistently throughout the 1960s, and one of the rewards of living in London at that time was the chance of seeing, singly or in bulk, the sculptures with which he closed one such gap after another. The steps in his development have not been seen in America where there has yet to be a museum show comparable to Caro's retrospectives at Whitechapel (1963) and the Hayward Gallery (1969). But he has been showing biennially at the Emmerich Gallery since 1964, and for his current show there he has sent over a batch of five new pieces. One at least of these, *Deep North* [45], is as important a piece as has been seen in the U.S. since *Span* (1966) [27] was shown in the 'American Sculpture in the Sixties' exhibition in Los Angeles and Philadelphia in 1967.

Deep North (1969–70) is a difficult piece: difficult to make, difficult to take in, difficult to elucidate. Seen with the eye of history, it could be said to have emerged quite logically from Caro's work of the 1960s. In 1960–61, he was out to get away from the totemic axis which was taken for granted by most sculptors at that time; he was against sculpture which sat up on a plinth and asked to be looked at; and he was against materials that 'had too much art-history in them': bronze, fine woods and marbles or steel and iron that had gone over to art and expected to be treated like precious metals. Whence the pieces which kept close to the ground were made up of materials with no previous esthetic connotations, and made visible an extremely complex series of relationships with means that were almost comically simple. Something in these works of 1960–61 can be related to Rodin's figure of *Earth*: a barely human shape, no more than adumbrated by the standards of Rodin's day, caught in the moment of hoisting itself clear of the primeval slime. In such pieces Rodin showed himself ready 'to let it happen': to allow what needed to be said to take priority, in other words, over what was then supposed to be sayable.

By 1962 Caro had mastered the ground to such an extent that he was able to work with branched aerial structures which barely touched the ground at all: the sculptures made their own earth and their own sky and went about their private business somewhere in between.

From having been as plain, bleak and blunt as it is possible for sculpture
to be, they gradually moved towards the dandified pieces of 1965–6:
these relate to the work of 1960–61 as the fine-boned daughters of a
second-generation millionaire relate to a grandsire who was all
thrust, ram and armored ambition. One could not exaggerate the elegance with which such pieces make their point; but the point is
never merely precious; something is said about the relation of one form
to another, or about the extent to which epigram can say more than
epic, which is equally relevant to our relations with ourselves, and with
others.

When Caro went back, around 1966, to making large complex and
compound structures, he was able to combine this elegance of statement
with the capacity to 'let it happen'. At a time when much that passed for sculpture was a matter of licensed attitudinizing on the one hand,
or bald non-resonant single forms on the other, Caro produced some
of the richest, firmest, most delicate and yet most virile statements that
the art of any period has had to show. An important factor in all
this is, I think, what can best be called the element of English discretion
in the work: and of English tolerance, also. Given a complex situation, Caro never aims to simplify it beyond a certain point. Nor does he
aim to 'make a Caro' on every possible occasion. If he has to choose
between an evident homogeneity and an untidied profusion, he chooses
profusion. In England, that is: for there is no doubt that the work he
did in Bennington, Vermont, in 1964–5, shows a marked tendency to
condense and polish and simplify. A piece like *Titan* (1964) [40] exemplifies, to my eye, the 'American look' in his work: fewer forms, larger
units, an altogether plainer and more finite kind of statement. In his
American years (his years of residence, that is to say; Caro still maintains
contacts with the U.S. which are as close as any ever enjoyed by an
English artist) his was an art of first principles, resolutely enunciated; in
England, idiosyncrasy is allowed its place.

Caro said late in 1965 that 'much of the sculpture I'm doing is about
extension': and for several years he did make, from time to time,
pieces which were, in this sense, 'about' the idea of extension or of levels,
or of line. The idea-piece *par excellence* was probably *Prairie* (1967)
[43], which is about all kinds of things, but primarily about horizontality:
and, in a more metaphorical way, about freedom – to exist in a grand,
open, explicit way that reverses the accepted conditions of life. Nothing
could go further, in technical terms, in the direction of an achieved
flatness and levelness and a definitive linearity. The natural place to go
after *Prairie* was 'overhead'. He had done all that he could do about

the ground, for the time being, and he had done all that he could do with the idea of horizontality: verticality was due for its turn, and in *Whispering*, a piece not yet shown anywhere, it got it.

A word about materials: for several years now Caro has been working with a cache of 37 tons of steel which was shipped to London, at Kenneth Noland's suggestion, from the late David Smith's studio at Bolton Landing. The experience of this prompted him to buy the group of monumental tank-ends which was used as the basic element in *After Summer* (1968) [36A, B]. (The Smith hoard also includes material not yet used but intrinsically very tempting: a group of stainless steel tubes, for instance.) For *Deep North* Caro used part of a tank-end that had been needed for *After Summer*, and a piece of the heavy-wire mesh which he had been using in 1966 to stand for forms which are both 'there' and not there; and he used fragments of a plow (which was invented some years ago for a crack-brained agricultural venture in what was then British Africa). But he also wished to thicken the plot by getting into the piece something of looseness and something of eloquent flow.

These qualities are of course contrary to the nature of steel; and as Caro also wanted the steel, at another point in *Deep North*, to peel away from itself as the skin peels away from a banana, it can be inferred that he has come a long way from the pieces of just ten years ago, in which steel units are put side by side, or on top of one another, without artifice or adaptation. These new forms of expression are part of a general new ambition: to try to portray the process of change instead (as in the earlier work) of portraying change itself. Caro produced a downhill, serpentine look with the help of some decrepit airplane propellers (which he bought for 60 cents apiece from de Havilland); for the peeling away of one piece of steel from another he used the plow-fragments, plus some heroic pioneering on the part of his technical assistant Charles Hendy.

Deep North seems to me to break down, in a way long unfamiliar in Caro's work, into two complementary areas. There is the vertical one, which has to do with what could be called 'over-the-topness'. In this, a rectangle of steel mesh is cantilevered above our heads and the propeller, somewhat widened for the purpose, introduces the downward-spiral motive. Complementary to this area is the horizontal one, in which the soft-looking spoon- or tongue-shaped forms peel away from another. One area is upright, the other spread-eagled; one speaks for engineering, the other for a kind of post-coital disarray which is quite new in Caro's work. (I do not, by the way, have his authority for these interpretations.) It belongs to the canon of Caro's larger, more complex, more openly exploratory work, and it stands for a very firm refusal to 'make another Caro'.

He is aware, meanwhile, of a tendency for the work to go in the direction of what he calls 'real shape' as against the *idea* of shape; *Deep North* exemplifies this by the way in which intractable shapes, and shapes not previously found in his work, are made to fit together. Caro is an open man and, in the old non-political sense, a pragmatic man: one who takes each experience as it comes. During the year in which Leonardo's drawings were on view in great numbers at the Queen's Gallery in London he made a piece (not sent to New York) which to my eye came very near to paraphrasing one of Leonardo's *Deluge* drawings; and as he has always had pinned up on his studio wall a tearsheet of Matisse standing in front of a late cut-out, I don't think it can be altogether false to see in his recent *Orangerie* [44] a reference to the seraphic vegetable-forms which Matisse cut out with his shears.

And yet the Leonardesque piece comes from Caro's having taken the curved forms which figure in many of his sculptures and given them, as it were, 'the run of the dump'; and the echoes of Matisse in *Orangerie* are incidental to its adroit mingling of two favorite themes of Caro's own – the table-top on which things happen, and the use of the ground as a kind of trampoline. In the last few years Caro has made nearly one hundred small pieces which sit half on and half off the table, inhabiting thereby a kind of between-world which is a new conquest for sculpture. These pieces are independent of any particular table and can be set down on any flat surface that is a little way above the ground; it is the peculiarity of *Orangerie* that it incorporates a flat plane that serves as an actual table-top, while on and around it individual forms (many of them drawn from the plows which were cannibalized for part of *Deep North*) are seen to be limbering up like dancers at the bar.

The new pieces are quite distinct from one another, but they have in common a characteristic of all Caro's successful work: they do not demand for their fulfilment that we should be looking at them. They are closed-circuit energy-systems, complete in themselves. Caro has gone on saying what needs to be said, and what could not be said in the language already available; but in a piece like *Deep North* he is as far as ever from saying it with one eye on the audience. The pieces are uncontaminated.   [1970]

Phyllis Tuchman: An Interview with Anthony Caro

Are the intentions of your figurative sculptures
related to your recent work?

My figurative sculptures were to do with what it's like to be inside the
body. That means, what it's like to be sitting in this chair, or lying
down flat, how it feels to smile. For example, when you're lying down,
you feel heavy; your weight causes you to feel flattened and pressed
down. The figurative sculptures were about this sort of thing. But all sculpture in some way has to do with the body. For instance, my sculptures now are partly dependent upon the spectator's height from the
floor when he is standing up: on his vertical stance, his consciousness of
flat ground. Sculptors and architects are necessarily conscious of the
body – it's very important. I've never wanted to take sculpture right out
of reality into the realm of illusion, out of thingness, weight or physicality. I don't necessarily want to call attention all the time to sculpture's
physicality, but I am forced to take these qualities into account, just
as the painter cannot ignore the qualities of *his* medium.

Is the acknowledgment of mass and weight
crucial for achieving a floating quality?

All sculptors have dreams of defying gravity. One of the inherent qualities
about sculpture is its heaviness, its substance. There is an attraction in
the dream of putting heavy pieces calmly up in the air and getting them to
stay there. I have tried to do this, for example, in *Month of May* [13].
But later I realized that if you can make the floor act as part of the sculpture and not just the base, then the pieces will float and move any-
way. In *Prairie* [43], the tubing appears to float, just extending into the
air. I would like to make sculptures that are more abstract. Sculpture
of its nature is not as abstract as painting. The sculptor's problem right
now, I think, is to make sculpture more abstract than it has been
before. In the last few years, sculpture became more anonymous in order
to get away from the tyranny of materials. And the treatment and
paint surface all gave it a blandness. Right now, I wonder if sculpture
could gain impetus from more feeling for material, possibly for
materials that haven't much been associated with it – string or paper,
for example. Making sculpture more abstract doesn't necessarily
take away its reality, its stuffness.

49 *(overleaf)*. Georgiana (first stage). 1969–70

Do you evaluate
your sculptures considering their appearance
indoors and outside?
I don't really evaluate a sculpture once I've finished it because that is to
do with being a critic and not a sculptor; at a certain point in the
making of a sculpture my own evaluation stops, and then the work can
stand on its own. Monet's art and David Smith's are examples of the
gain to one's work of keeping the momentum going.

Of course there are some wrong settings for sculpture. Just as it would
be meaningless to play a quartet in a marketplace so there are some
quite unsuitable sites for certain sculptures. I prefer my sculpture to be
seen in a tranquil and enclosed space. Almost all sculpture, I guess,

needs to be indoors – or enclosed in some way; it mostly blows away if it's in the open air, or else it becomes environment. To get post-Renaissance sculpture to hold its own outdoors, it has to be really differently conceived and a sculpture which could hold its own outside a skyscraper hasn't been made yet, so far as I know. There are architectural squares in Venice which hold space almost like a room, where even a flagpole looks right sculpturally. But modern sculptures would look wrong in those settings because the sculptures are not architectural in a Renaissance sense, either in scale or concept. It would be necessary to think about the problem quite freshly. Certainly, just blowing existing sculpture up big would not meet the case at all. For my part, up to now, all my sculpture (however large) is un-public.

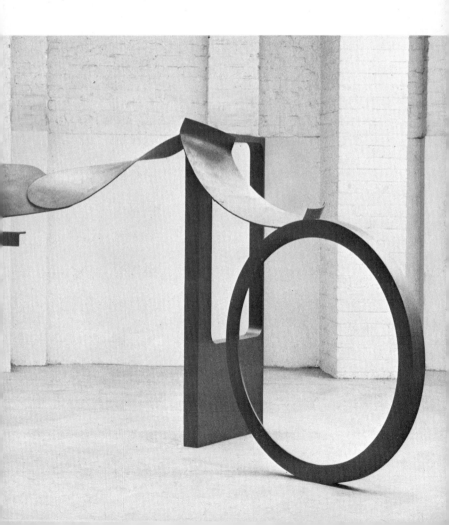

*Do you have any objections to a spectator's experiencing one of your
sculptures by walking into it and over it, when they can?*
Yes, I do. When it's sculpture, it's to be looked at. Sculpture, for me, is
something outside of which you are. It's not something you can get
inside; it's not architecture or environment. I put this limit on sculpture
and I think that by so doing, I gain more freedom, not less. Every
generation allows for sculpture or painting a little different theater of
operations than before. And all new art at the time it is made is
about going as close to the edge as possible, but without losing one's
foothold. So we extend our limits and take our risks, but not without caution. In this way, all control doesn't get lost.

50. *Cadenza*, 1970

Without walking around a sculpture,
wouldn't you lose
the necessary viewpoints?

You didn't say around, you said walking into: walking into a building
and walking around a building are different. Walking around my
sculptures is important, at the very least, even if only because it gives
knowledge of widths or thicknesses. But I don't recommend my
sculpture be looked at as one looks at a sculpture built volumetrically
around a central core. There are films where a fixed camera shows
such a sculpture turning and each frame reveals a new aspect – the pace
of change here is too steady for my work.

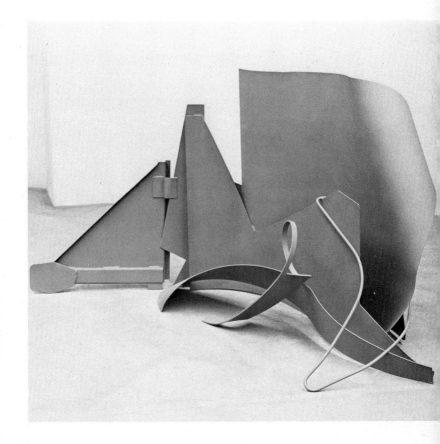

51. *Crown*, 1970–71

Do you distinguish between
a sculpture's size and scale and their relationship
to the spectator?
The old statue was made on a base and it inhabited a world of its own,
the limits of which were set by the limits of its base. Whether it was
an equestrian statue or a little model on a piano or a mantelpiece, it inhabited its own world. I don't want my sculpture to relate to the
spectator in this imaginary sort of way. It has to do with presence, more
as one person relates to another.

52. *Paul's Turn,* 1971

53. *Side Step*, 1971

When you speak of a sculpture of abstraction,
does that mean an art devoid of content?

Is orchestral or chamber music devoid of content because it's more abstract than opera or love songs? Your question is such an old and tired one; I can only answer by repeating what has been said many times before, and in a hundred different ways. In sculpture and painting and music, whether figurative or abstract, feelings and moods are somehow implied and the sensibilities of the artist are reflected in the work. The art that I prefer is that in which intelligence and sensuality are both given rein. I aim in my work for the form and content, problem-solving and expression to be so integrated that they are indivisible. And the meaning should be right there in the sculptural expression.

54. *Focus*, in construction, 1971

In the beginning, did you
use color to unify pieces because they had, say,
different shapes and different weights?

In 1959 or 1960, I wanted my sculpture to look straightforward: no art
props, no nostalgia, no feelings of the preciousness associated with
something because it's old or bronze, or it's rusty, encrusted, or patinated.
So I just covered it with a coat of paint. I used brown or black paint
and the sculptures looked more as if they were destined for a locomotive
factory than an art gallery. Later, I found the browns and blacks
rather drab, and so I experimented with other colors and I found that
they often helped to emphasize the mood of the work.

55. *Up Front,* 1971

*Have you ever found
that you emphasize rectilinearity
rather than curvilinear forms?*

I think perhaps I am attracted to each at different times. The rococo
lyricism and flamboyance of curves are dangerous because they can take
possession of a sculpture. Answering curves and licks leads straight
into sheer design. Similarly, so can that neat rectangle be a bad master.
But they're all bad masters, those things: it's like being trapped by a
style. Style has just nothing to do with art – it's the intent that counts.

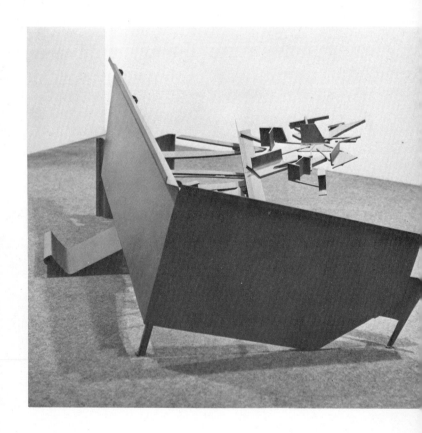

56. *Cherry Fair*, 1971

Do you find that after working
on large-size sculpture, it's a relief
doing smaller ones?

Yes, I treat the small ones like that. Maybe they're like drawings. I often make them in the evenings when I have been at work during the day on something large. I like to vary the size. Getting to know how one works well in the studio and learning to go with that rhythm is a very important part of the business of making art.

57. *Straight Cut,* 1972

58. *Straight Up*, 1972

59. *Straight On*, 1972

*Do you ever consider your sculptures as relating
to the idea of drawing in space?*
If by drawing in space you mean essentially a two-dimensional approach,
then the answer is no, I almost never start working from a flat beginning; but I am interested in exploring space in a free, unconstrained way.
As it happens, my training as a student emphasized that one perceived
sculptural shape in the way that your hand holds a pebble, and I think
there's still some consciousness of implied volume in the flattest, most
silhouetted works I've made.

60. *Cool Deck,* 1971

If you were working on a sculpture
in a room small enough so that you couldn't back away,
how did you get it out the door?

That's a practical thought. If they were very big, they were always bolted. All my sculpture of any size has to be in pieces because it is supported over a considerable distance of ground. Unlike a vertical construction which rests on a small area, once a heavy, loosely joined horizontal object no longer has the support of the ground, it's impossible to move it in one piece. Obviously you can't just pick it up and carry it away because it's the ground which normally does the work. For that reason, I bolt it in as many places as is needed and dismantle and remount it.

61. *Table Piece CXX*, 1973

The advantage of making them where I couldn't stand back from them was that I used this limitation to prevent my falling back on my previous knowledge of balance and composition. That's not new. Kenneth Noland told me in 1959 how he painted on the floor and on sawhorses for the same reason. Working in a one-car garage as I used to do was a way of trying to force my mind to accept a new sort of rightness that I wanted – I had to refrain from backing away and editing the work prematurely. When I took the work outside, it was a shock sometimes insofar as it looked different from sculpture that I was accustomed to. So I was able to discover something and that's what I wanted to do. But this business of discovery is what making art is about, and this is where most of the fun lies. [1972]

62. *Table Piece CXVI,* 1973

More about Penguins and Pelicans

Penguinews, which appears every month, contains details of all the new
books issued by Penguins as they are published. From time to time
it is supplemented by *Penguins in Print,* which is a complete list of all
available books published by Penguins. (There are well over four
thousand of these.)

A specimen copy of *Penguinews* will be sent to you free on request. For a
year's issues (including the complete lists) please send 30p if you
live in the United Kingdom, or 60p if you live elsewhere. Just write to
Dept EP, Penguin Books Ltd, Harmondsworth, Middlesex, enclosing
a cheque or postal order, and your name will be added to the mailing list.

Note: *Penguinews* and *Penguins in Print* are not available in the U.S.A.
or Canada

Penguin New Art

The following quarto editions of Penguin New Art are still available with their lavish illustrations in colour.

Robyn Denny *by David Thompson*

Born in Surrey in 1930 Denny has had numerous one-man exhibitions in many countries and has also had his work on display in group exhibitions in New York, Venice and elsewhere. Among others the Peter Stuyvesant Foundation, the Tate Gallery and the British Council all possess examples of his art.

Claes Oldenburg *by Ellen H. Johnson*

Though Swedish by birth Oldenburg was brought up in the United States and received his art training there. His sculpture has been widely exhibited since 1958. His imagery of commonplace and often vastly enlarged objects, monuments and projections for monuments has given him the reputation of a 'pop' artist. There is, however, subtlety and formal complexity in his work and he has in particular enlisted a whole range of new materials in the cause of sculpture.

Also available

Patrick Caulfield *by Christopher Finch*
Frank Stella *by Robert Rosenblum*